The Monster's Lap

Drew Bankston

Dedication

To all of the brave family members, parents and grandparents who work so hard to protect the innocent children in their families and for the strength of making it through being the second victims.

-Drew.

Forward

Sex is a part of the basic human drive to recreate and keep our species alive. Without sex, we would cease to exist. It can be a pleasurable thing and a sign of love and affection between two people, but sex without mutual consent can be a devastating event, not only for the person being violated but also for that person's friends, family, and other loved ones. When the person being molested is a child, it is especially heinous, particularly when the child trusts the perpetrator and doesn't really know the meaning of what is going on. When a child only feels this is wrong and is confused by the actions, it can have long-lasting consequences, reaching many years into that child's future. This is a stark reminder of the urgency of addressing sexual abuse, underscoring the need for immediate action. You are about to read the true story of one such event and how this unimaginable and selfish act on the part of one adult changed not only a child's life but also so many others' lives. Come with me on this journey of several months and see how my family received the help and support of community officials and those around us while helping to heal our little girl and ourselves. A warning. Many letters are included from the perpetrator, but these are unedited and may be difficult to read emotionally. Please use discretion before continuing on.

CHAPTER 1

The Father

❖

My name is Stephen Bolton. I've lived a long life, and during that time, I've seen a lot of pain and suffering, sadness, and despair. I believe I've done what I could to be kind and help people when they've needed help.

I've always believed in Karma and thought that what goes around comes around, so I expected my life to run smoothly. I never expected my life to be torn apart by one smart assed kid who would have the nerve to hurt a member of my family and then deny it. Sorry, I tend to get ahead of myself. Let me go back.

When I got married, it was a fantastic day. I was finally committed to the woman of my dreams. We were going to raise a family! We didn't waste much time; before you knew it, we had a daughter. Now, I'm not one to sit around, and by golly, as time went by, we had six of the cutest kids you could ever hope for. Time does strange things, though, and even though Carla, she's my wife, and I worked our tails off to make a good life for them, things started to happen. Those strange things only seem to happen when kids become teens. But instead of boring you and rambling, let me let you read for yourself. I'll just jump in if something needs explaining from time to time.

My oldest daughter, Sharon, was interested in boys. I guess these days, that's a hit or miss for many kids! Anyway, she brought several young men home, and her choice of partners didn't impress me. She had just returned from shopping and had another young man with her. Here's how our first meeting went.

"Daddy," Sharon said, slightly pushing the young man toward me, "this is Larry."

The young man stuck out his hand. "How do you do, sir," he said, shaking my hand.

I looked this kid over. Inside, I couldn't help but chuckle as I thought Larry looked like someone had dressed up a Cabbage Patch Kid in western wear. He continued to shake my hand, and I noticed how soft it was. Not the hand you would expect from a cowboy. "Nice to meet you, Larry," I said warmly, but only for my daughter's sake. "So, you're a cowboy?"

"Yes, sir," Larry answered with a slight drawl.

I have lived almost everywhere in the country, but I wasn't sure exactly where Larry's drawl came from. I figured I'd ask Sharon later to avoid embarrassing the boy.

"My grandfather owned a ranch. I loved him more than anyone. He almost raised me," Larry said reverently.

"Is that right?" I replied, impressed at the respect that Larry had for his grandfather.

"Yes, sir," he said. "He taught me how to work hard and respect women."

I felt a little more relieved, but only a little. I couldn't help but think that maybe my daughter had finally found a guy to treat her right, but something still bothered me about Larry. It was something that I couldn't quite put my finger on. Was it really something, or was it the protective father part of me ready to strike?

I know you're just getting into the story, and I apologize for interrupting you. Still, I want you to understand something about my wife and I. We always wanted our kids to grow up in the perfect world. Each of our children would be smart and funny and procure good jobs while enjoying a family. Carla and I would then be free to enjoy the benefits of grandkids. The families would visit often, laugh, and talk about the fun of growing up in a happy home.

My oldest daughter, Sharon, was the first of three girls and three boys to grace our household. Now, I certainly have my opinion on which sex is easier to raise. If I were to say it out loud, Carla might disagree with me, depending on the child, so I never bring up that particular discussion. Each of our children was different in different ways, and they remain so to this day!

We've both always thought Sharon was a beautiful baby who grew up to become a beautiful young woman. Parents are always proud of their kids and love it when they receive validation from others outside of the family. Honestly, we are not excluded from that club, and we always smile each time someone confirms how beautiful our daughter is.

We had always attempted to instill self-confidence and intelligence in our children. I found out, however, that you can encourage numerous traits in your children. Still, they have to develop other characteristics on their own. Anyway, Sharon was a beautiful young lady and, at sixteen years old, had fallen into a relationship with a young man who apparently was worth sneaking out at night for. Once Sharon was caught and spoken with, and caught again by the police bringing her home, it came out that the young man she had been seeing had not only raped her but was also physically abusive to her.

If you're not a father, you might not understand how wanting to hurt someone who hurt your little girl makes any sense. When you reach the age where you realize that violence doesn't help in a violent situation, but cunning thinking does, then you've reached a new level of revenge. So, I found a way to keep them apart and maintain my freedom. Still, the die had been cast and Sharon would forever use this first experience as a role model for the type of person she wanted. This would not go well as the years went by.

To continue, a few other boyfriends came and went, many of them troublemakers or in and out of prison. It wasn't until the boyfriend that Carla and I referred to as "The Slug" came along that things started to really take a turn. Yes, The Slug was Larry, not the cowboy he attempted to portray.

I've always been trusting. I guess it's just always been in my nature to trust people. Even if something terrible happens, I quickly forgive and offer second chances. That leads me back to Larry. So now you can get on with the story.

As days passed, Larry came over frequently and helped around the house. I was happy to see it and appreciated the help.

I was incredibly thankful for Larry's presence when an accident happened in my family.

Carla and I went to dinner at a local restaurant, which Carla particularly enjoyed. We laughed and had a wonderful meal when Carla excused herself to head to the restroom. On her way there, she slipped on a wet spot in front of the hostess' station and fell on her knee. Later that night, Carla and I went into the emergency room after Carla's knee had swollen to the size of a grapefruit. The doctor said that she had some damage to the cartilage in her knee and that she would need to be off of it for several weeks. No driving.

I became the taxi driver, chief cook, and bottle washer for the family.

My boss at work was somewhat understanding and adjusted my schedule accordingly. However, my back went out in the middle of all of this. A great deal of work was to be done in the yard, and I turned to Larry for help.

Larry didn't have a job. He did, however, have great plans for his future, and as I listened to Larry's plans, I started to realize what bothered me. Larry's dreams were just that. Dreams. Larry wanted to be a Game Programmer and spent his days studying to be the "great one" by playing video games, sometimes until the early morning hours. He also aspired to be a police officer and hoped to attend the local academy someday. However, that was where it ended, with Larry only dreaming about these things. He would avoid talking about how he would reach these goals.

"Someday, I'll make thirty dollars an hour," he would say.

"Are you planning on going to school to study criminal justice or computer programming?" I asked.

"I'm looking into it, but I don't know where I want to go," Larry would reply. "I need to find the very best school. I hope to find a school with programming and some pre-police training programs. Then I can go to the academy or go into game programming for some huge company."

"That might be something to look into more earnestly. You'll need that criminal justice background before applying for the academy."

"Yeah," Larry would say, "but being a game programmer pays more." Then he would walk away.

.

"I'm wondering if you could help me with something," I said as I stopped thinking about Larry's inability to find a goal worthy of his attention and focused on the young man before me.

"Sure," Larry replied, "what can I do?"

"There's a lot of work to get done in the backyard, and I'm wondering if you would mind helping with it. Sharon could help as well. I'll fix you meals, but I'm afraid I really can't pay you."

I knew that Larry loved to eat and appreciated my cooking. Larry lived with his grandmother and didn't have much for bills. This should have been a red flag, but I knew people occasionally fell on hard times, so I didn't think much about it.

"That's fine, sir," Larry said. "I'm happy to help."

For me, this was all part of the roller coaster ride of emotions about Larry. For Carla, there was no roller coaster.

"There's just something about him that I don't like," Carla would say. "He's lazy, and I just don't like him."

"He's going to help in the backyard," I said. "That's got to mean something." I knew deep down, however, that she was right. I was hoping that she was, maybe, mistaken.

"It means he gets to spend time with Sharon," Carla said, wincing from the pain in her knee. "We'll see how long this lasts."

It didn't take long for me to see Carla's intuitive feelings come to fruition.

On the first day, Larry did an outstanding job and worked very hard. I felt so bad that I couldn't help out, but the spasms in my back made it difficult for me to walk, let alone lift, bend, or carry anything. I became as miserable as Carla on both a physical and emotional level.

The second day, I looked out of the back window and saw Larry frequently taking breaks by leaning against the fence or sitting on the ground talking to Sharon.

On the third day, Larry slowed down, complained a lot, and worked little, if any, until it finally stopped altogether. Larry found excuses not to work, and I just let it go, feeling bad for not being able to do it all myself. I also felt terrible because Carla was right.

As time passed, I found more and more reasons to dislike Larry. I knew that my daughter was about to turn eighteen and felt she was heading toward moving in with Larry. In my mind and heart, it seemed like a short step off of a big cliff, and I wondered how much of this feeling was dislike for the young man and how much of it was the father's instinct to not let my daughter go. I thought about Larry and tried to see him in a good light, but each time I did, I cringed at the thought of Sharon living with this boy.

Regardless of what I thought, however, I felt it was inevitable. I hoped that if I allowed Sharon to go early, she would miss her family and the comforts of her home and decide to move back.

Even though Larry lived with his grandmother in a mobile home, if Sharon moved in with him, they would have to move out into the camper that rested in grandma's backyard—not even a camper as much as a camper shell.

"Sharon, can I talk to you for a moment?" I said, feeling uncomfortable at the impending conversation.

"Sure, Daddy," Sharon said, stepping into his home office.

"It's getting close to your birthday. I'm assuming that you plan on moving in with Larry when you turn eighteen."

"Yeah," she replied. "I was thinking about it."

"I thought so," I said thoughtfully and sadly. "If it's inevitable, you might as well begin moving there now."

Sharon looked shocked. "Really? Okay. Thank you, Daddy."

I couldn't tell if she was pleased or confused. I felt that it was the latter. "I just figure that if you're going to do it, you'll do it whether your mom and I give you permission to go or not."

Sharon was quiet.

Carla and I had three cars. The third car, our van, was old and had some issues, but it could be fixed. "We'd like to give you and Larry the van," I told Sharon. "Larry is always saying that he would like to fix it up. I know you don't have your driver's license yet, but at least you two could have a reliable vehicle once he fixes it. It would be better than him buying an old pick-up truck and trying to restore it on your income like he always says he wants to do."

Larry fancied himself the world's most incredible auto mechanic and was always looking at old pick-up trucks to try and buy so that he could make them his dream truck. This, of course, never happened, but the dream remained alive. I wondered what it was like to constantly live in a dream world. I didn't think that I could do it.

"That would be great. Thank you daddy," Sharon said.

The next few weeks were difficult for both Carla and I. Larry would come over and work on the van. I knew now that Larry knew nothing about what he was doing, even though I had given him a repair manual for the van and loaned him the tools to get the job done. Interestingly enough, those tools I had loaned Larry to fix the van eventually disappeared. I firmly believe that they went to a good pawnshop instead of a good home, but Karma had a way of handling these things, and I knew that eventually, Larry would learn that.

I helped Larry work on the van whenever possible, but I wanted him to show his true colors. When I finally got the van running, Sharon and Larry used it to move the larger items belonging to Sharon out of the house. Like a clap of thunder, her presence faded away, and to the dismay of Carla and me, she was out on her own.

There was a lot of worry as winter came, and Carla and I would hear about how the camper let the cold in. The electric heater run with an extension cord from Grandma's trailer was a worry. The fact that Larry still didn't have a job was a worry. The fact that Sharon was overdrawing her bank account was a worry. Hearing that Larry would invite a few of his friends to stay the night with all of them in the camper was a worry, although I thought it might create more warmth. Still, I wanted to step in and end it all, but Sharon was eighteen, and I couldn't force her to come home. I could only give care packages and show my support while slipping in my concerns. I wasn't sure what to do except let fate take its course and wait for the moment I could do something.

When Sharon started talking about how sick she was feeling and how nauseous she was all the time, Carla started asking if she was pregnant, but every time she asked, the answer would always be "No."

After Sharon moved out, things went downhill for Carla, me, and our family. Because of the high hospital debt and the fact that I had lost my job when my part-time schedule didn't suit my employer's needs, we had to move out of our house and into a mobile home. As we started to get back on our feet, we were able to find a house to rent. It was after we had moved into this house that we heard the news that Carla had suspected was causing Sharon's constant illness. Sharon was pregnant.

Carla conceded that she was excited to become a grandmother and started buying baby items for the new addition. She even planned a baby shower, which several of Sharon's old friends attended. Things were going better.

I no longer communicated with Larry but did help Sharon and Larry move from the camper to a house they had found to rent. It wasn't the best house in the county but was a step up from the camper. I was in for another surprise when I spoke with Sharon about the house.

"We have our own bedroom downstairs," she said, "but we're sharing the house with another couple."

"Friends of yours?" I asked.

"Yeah," Sharon said uncomfortably. "I think that they're having some relationship problems, though."

"Oh?" I said. "What kind of problems?"

"Well, he's been in and out of jail for some kind of drug charges, and I think his wife, or girlfriend, or whatever she is, is taking their child and leaving him."

I was speechless. Inside, I was furious. I didn't know what to do. I wanted to be supportive. I wanted to pick Sharon up, carry her away, and talk some sense into her. I didn't know what to say. I didn't know what I could say. I hugged my daughter. "If you need anything, just let us know." I didn't feel good about leaving, but I would keep an eye on things from a distance, as fathers tend to do. However, I was concerned about what might happen once the new baby was born. I just thought about the dream of having my family healthy and happy. I didn't believe this would happen in this situation, which tore me up.

CHAPTER 2

The Arrival

❖

Eventually, the fateful day arrived, and the baby was born. It was a fantastic day. All of the family crowded into the hospital room. My mom was there to visit her great-granddaughter. Carla's mom and dad came to see the new arrival. Even the new aunts and uncles came to have the chance to hold the tiny little girl. Sharon was thrilled, as was Larry, although whenever I look back at the photos, I realize that Larry never smiled in a single one. It reminded me of the old-time photos where no one in the family smiled; it was just Larry. Everyone else smiled and laughed and enjoyed the moment of new life. Sharon named the new bundle of joy Julie.

As Julie grew, she was given gifts of clothing, food, and toys from grandma, grandpa, and many others. The summer came and went. Fall was uneventful but cute when Sharon and Julie came over with Julie's first Halloween costume. Carla and I were getting information about Larry from Sharon about how he was still only playing video games. We heard how Larry would become so involved in his games that sometimes he would forget to change Julie's diaper during the day. Sharon would get home from work, and Larry expected her to care for Julie, which she would do while he continued to conquer his imaginary lands. It made me furious, even more so when, no matter what I would say in the form of hints or suggestions, they would go unheeded by Sharon, and life would continue.

As winter set in, Carla and I heard some disturbing news from Sharon about their living conditions.

"They shut off our water," Sharon told them, "but our roommate cut the lock and turned it back on. We pay him money for the utilities, but I guess it never reaches the companies. He spends it on other things."

"This needs to stop!" I would say, about reaching the end of my rope.

But it wasn't until I had heard that the gas had been turned off and that they had been using the electric kitchen stove to warm the house that Carla and I took action.

"They had left the stove on to heat the house, and it melted to the vent hood," Sharon told them, "but I think that our roommate is going to cut the lock and turn the gas back on, too."

"You're going to lose your child if this keeps up," I told her. If the authorities find out what the living conditions are like, then they'll take Julie away from you. I'm sure they will find out if the bills are unpaid and the locks are continually cut off. The utility companies will eventually catch on and send the police out. Anyone on the lease will be liable for the past-due bills and the fines involved with stealing water and gas."

"You need to pack up your belongings and come here to live with us," Carla said. You can stay in the front room on the couch since we don't have any extra bedrooms. At least you'll be warm and have food. Larry is not welcome."

Sharon gathered her belongings in garbage bags, got Julie, and moved in with her parents. Larry wasn't happy, but he really didn't have a choice at that point. He filled his days by continuing to play his video games.

I didn't like Larry much at all now and was sure I knew where my power tools had disappeared when Larry helped us move garage things from the house. Sharon occasionally told me that Larry had contributed money by pawning one thing or another. Still, she wasn't sure what he had been pawning.

For the longest time, I thought that I had perhaps misplaced my power tools during one of the many moves that we had to make, but now I guessed that I'd be saving up to buy new ones sometime in the future and that the missing power tools were gone forever.

Larry rarely found time to come visit his daughter or his girlfriend. When he wanted to meet, they would meet at the mall, where Larry spent more time trying to get his girl back than he did visiting with his daughter. Larry only wanted someone to care for him and bring in money. Sharon told him that if he wanted things to work out, he needed to prove to her that he could get a job and care for his family. His attempts were feeble at best. He would get and hold a job for a month or so before he was fired or quit. Carla and I were very relieved that Larry and Sharon had never married.

Sharon stayed with us for several months, and we absolutely loved having both her and our granddaughter with us.

We were present at Julie's first word and her first steps. It was a wonderful time.

One day, Sharon announced she had a new boyfriend and told us how good he was to her and Julie. Both of us were surprised but hopeful, and when the young man finally came over, we met him for the first time.

"I'm Richard," the young man said.

I shook his hand and was impressed with his smile, firm handshake, and confident air. I remembered the first time that I met Larry, and I was wary, but I still had a trust for people, and I gave Richard a chance.

Over the next few days, Richard worked his way into my heart, but not so with Carla. Carla felt something not quite right about Richard.

I worked on Richard's car. He actually asked for my help. One day, he became serious when we were working on the brakes.

"I wanted to let you know that I have a past," Richard said.

"We all do," I replied, trying hard to release a stuck bolt. "What did you want to tell me about yours?"

"Well," Richard started uneasily, "I wanted you to know some things about me, and I wanted you to hear them from me. I'm not proud of some of these things, but I want to explain what happened."

I felt a mix of uneasy feelings, curiosity, and suspicion. "Go ahead," I encouraged and continued working on the car brakes.

"I wanted you to know that I have a criminal history."

I stopped working on the brakes and looked at Richard. What the hell was going to be revealed now?

"Oh?" I said. "What did you do?" I chose not to look at Richard but returned to working on the stubborn bolt. It gave me something else to focus on.

"Well," Richard started, "I was charged with having sex with a minor." Before I could say anything, Richard continued. "It really wasn't my fault. I had just turned eighteen and met this girl. She had alcohol in her backpack, and she looked so much older. The next thing I knew, the police were taking her away as a runaway, and I didn't know what to do. It seemed that no one believed my story, even though the girl said that it was her fault. The DA pressed charges against me without the parents even pressing charges, and I had to spend some time in jail, even though the police admitted that she looked older than she was."

"That doesn't seem right," I said sympathetically. I meant it. Richard seemed so sincere that it was hard to doubt his story.

"I didn't think so either, but there was nothing I could do," Richard said. "You should also know that I'm being charged with domestic violence on another case."

"What?" I asked again.

"My ex-girlfriend and mother of my son was arguing with me. I tried calming her down, but she was getting really fired up. I went to take her by the shoulders to escort her out of the room, but she twisted away, and I accidentally scratched her neck. Because of that mark, I was charged with domestic violence. I wasn't trying to hurt her at all. I just thought she needed to leave and calm down."

"Wow. You don't have much luck with things," I said, putting my hand on Richard's shoulder. "Is there anything I can do to help?"

"No," Richard said sadly. "I just need to fight it and ensure that nothing like this happens again."

I sincerely felt bad for Richard and admired his forthcomingness about his past. I have always believed that we all have something in our pasts that we're not proud of. Most of the time, we choose not to reveal those little secrets.

Richard came over almost every day to visit Sharon and Julie. He would stay as late as he could but worked three nights each week at a bar and cooked for the same business at different times. I was delighted to see that Richard had a job and was a hard worker.

I wondered where Richard lived and asked Sharon about it.

"He doesn't have any place to live right now," she said, "so he stays in his car in the Walmart parking lot. Most of his money goes toward child support for his son."

The night was going to be cold, so I told Sharon that Richard was welcome to spend the night in the house with our family.

"I really appreciate you letting me crash on your couch," Richard said. Then, with tears in his eyes, he said, "I've never really had a family that cared about me before."

I felt good doing the right thing.

Richard stayed the night, where he was fed and continued working on his car. Carla and I talked about what I had learned about Richard's past.

"He was candid about his past. I really like that. He seemed very sincere," I said.

"He may have been honest, but do you really want someone like this around our daughter? Around our granddaughter?" Carla was upset.

"Why would he tell me all this if he thought we would tell him to stay away? He must have thought about that before telling me." I argued.

"Maybe he was hoping that you would think this way," Carla said. "I don't trust him. He has assault charges pending. What kind of a father will he be?"

"Maybe he's just a victim of circumstance," I said.

"I hope that you're right. In the meantime, I say we keep our guard up."

Richard stayed the next night and a few more after that. When we spoke next, he revealed another fact about his past.

"Because of the sexual assault issue, I had to register as a sex offender," Richard said.

"So, if you don't have a permanent address," I asked, "how do you keep the police informed?"

"I let them know where I am," Richard said matter-of-factly. "It's the law."

I thought for a moment. Richard's statement made me uncomfortable: "Do the police know you've been staying here?"

"This is just temporary," Richard said with a sigh. "I wish it was permanent, but I understand you don't have the room. I'm just really grateful that you let me stay."

"You do realize that we have a deputy sheriff as a neighbor, don't you?" I asked.

"I've seen the car over there. I don't want you to get into trouble because of me. I'll only stay a few nights and then sleep in my car a few nights so that no one questions you."

This phrasing bothered me, but I knew Richard was trying to look out for us, right? Still, Richard was more worried about the authorities bothering him and not so much about whether they bothered our family.

In August, we had to find another house to rent, as our current lease was up and our current home was too small for the family. Sharon, Richard, and Julie followed. Eventually, Richard was tried for the domestic violence charge and placed on work release. After a few weeks in work release, he was caught fighting. He claimed that it wasn't his fault and that he was actually trying to stop the fight, but bad luck, once again, intervened when they found alcohol in his car. This was a violation of his work release agreement. So, he was taken from work, released, and placed in jail. Richard claimed that the alcohol wasn't his and that the police had planted it. Yet another lousy twist of fate that didn't go in his favor.

Once Richard left jail, he moved back in with Sharon and her family. We had found a bigger house with more room, and Sharon, Richard, and Julie had a large main room downstairs to themselves. It was a temporary arrangement until Sharon could find a place in low-income housing where she and Julie could move. She was hoping that Richard could move with them, but she was having trouble finding any place that would allow Richard, given his past offenses.

My younger daughters sometimes complained that money was missing from their rooms during their stay. I tried to reason that perhaps they had misplaced their cash, but logic told me otherwise. My girls had never lost significant amounts of money at the same time without even taking it out of their rooms. The bad thing was that it only happened after Richard had supposedly slept alone in the house.

Since Julie was sleeping downstairs in her crib, she often would go to sleep to movies on Richard's laptop. When Sharon and Richard were at work, Carla had gone down once to start the movies for Julie. She had never used that laptop before and wasn't familiar with where the files were. Richard used it most of the time, and Carla used a Mac, so a PC laptop was somewhat foreign to her. She opened the screen and clicked on the media player. What came up shocked her as graphic pornography filled the screen, unseen by Julie. File after file popped up as photos and movies appeared. Carla finally got all of the screens closed and found where the Netflix movie files were located.

Richard often stayed up late at night and watched what he said was anime or played games. Carla thought she knew what Richard was really watching now when her daughter and granddaughter were sleeping.

Another time, Carla noticed that the downstairs looked rather shoddy and a complete mess. When Sharon was at work, she spoke with Richard about the state of the basement.

"Richard, the basement really needs to be picked up. It's getting to be quite the mess. We don't want mice down here, and with what's being left out, it's an open invitation," Carla said.

Richard sighed. "I've been getting on Sharon about picking up, but she just doesn't seem to listen. I'll talk to her again tonight when she gets home."

Carla was never aggressive, but she wished at that moment that she had the nerve to tell him that he wasn't doing anything during the day, so he should help.

Another time, Richard was supposed to be watching Julie downstairs. Carla was in the kitchen cooking when Richard came up to ask if there was anything he could do to help. She turned to look at him and noticed that he had earbuds and was listening to music.

She said, "Aren't you supposed to be watching Julie?"

He took out the earbuds and asked, "What?"

Carla went downstairs, but Julie was nowhere to be found. They looked and finally found her in another room, going through her toys. Carla looked at Richard, and he shrugged. He had no idea that she wasn't in the room. Carla was getting fed up with his irresponsibility.

Eventually, Sharon grew tired of living with her parents and hearing about the increases in the electric bill, Richard's unacceptable behavior, and other bills such as groceries and the need to pay rent. So she and Richard found another place to move to. A friend of Sharon's had offered them a room to bunk in for minimal rent. Off they went to be out in the world on their own. Richard rented a storage space where the couple shared the storage of their personal items that wouldn't be accommodated by the new and smaller space. The storage space wasn't the only thing that they started to share. Sharon put Richard on her auto insurance as well as his car. She also purchased a phone plan and put him on it. They were becoming closer, not only emotionally but also financially.

In February, the couple once again had to move when Sharon's friends had to leave their house. Sharon, Richard, and Julie moved back in with us, and we were all together once again.

I noticed that when there was work to be done, and Richard was asked to help, he couldn't even though he seemed like he wanted to. "My back is out," he would say, or "My leg hurts," and he would take out a cane. "I've been having seizures, and I'm not sure why," was another reason. I would finish the job myself and move on, but I was getting irritated with his excuses.

Finally, one day, Sharon came to Carla and was very excited. "I got a call from the housing authority," she said. "They have an apartment for me! It's on a sliding fee scale, so it will be perfect since I'm not working many hours right now."

"How big is the apartment?" Carla asked.

"It's a two-bedroom," Sharon said. "I can get the keys and look at it tomorrow. Do you want to come with me?"

"I'd love to see it, sweetheart," Carla said. She was proud that our daughter would be out on her own but worried about how she would get by with yet another bill to deal with. After Richard went to jail, he lost his job at the bar. He hadn't been able to find another since his release and spent much of his day sleeping so that he could watch anime and play games at night. Because of his record, it was difficult for him to find any jobs, so he continued to hope that he'd be able to get his job back at the bar eventually.

The next day, Carla and Sharon went to the apartment. Carla looked around. It reminded her a little of her and Stephen's first apartment: small, efficient, and inexpensive.

"You should have your father come take a look at it as well," Carla said. "He used to do maintenance for apartment complexes and would know what to look for that might need attention before you move in."

"Thank you, Mom," Sharon said, hugging her mom.

Over the next few days, I looked over the apartment. I wrote down things that Sharon should talk to management about and created my own 'walk-through' form for her. I was pleased that there were no major problems with the apartment, but I felt terrible that I didn't have the money to help my daughter find a better place. At least it was a roof over her head and a place for Julie. I asked about where Richard was going to live.

"He'll stay in his car most of the time or stay with friends. I'm going to let him stay with me sometimes so that he can shower and cook."

I didn't feel good about that, but I kept quiet. I really didn't want Sharon to not have a place to stay, and I wanted her to be happy. If the management discovered that Richard was staying there, I worried that Sharon might lose her home.

Sharon and Richard moved out of our house. I helped where and when I could, helping to move heavy furniture. Sharon's brother, Troy, also helped when he could and helped me move down some donated furniture provided by Carla's parents.

I noticed that it seemed a little lonelier without my oldest daughter in the house, but at the same time, I gave a sigh of relief. She was out on her own and ready to build a life of her own, and besides, I still had three more children to raise at home. Carla and I weren't empty nesters yet! However, my relief was short-lived when I realized that Richard was staying at Sharon's place much more than she originally said.

The holidays began rolling around, and I discovered that Richard's father, Bertran, was planning to visit. Richard's father was disabled and divorced from Richard's mother. He, however, still lived with her and relied on her for help and support. He could still walk and work online to make some extra money, helping Richard and Sharon whenever possible.

"Where is Bertran going to stay while he's up here?" I asked Sharon.

"He's going to stay at my place, on the couch," Sharon replied hesitantly.

"Why is he staying with you?" I asked.

"He really doesn't have anyplace else," she said, "and he wants to see Richard and Julie."

There wasn't much I could say except, "That's going to make it tight for you. Maybe you should invite Bertran to come over for Thanksgiving dinner here at our house. That way, you don't have to worry about cooking."

I absolutely love cooking and baking, and during the holiday season, I have the opportunity to show off those skills. I am also a compassionate man and have received a lot of help in the past when my family and I were in need. I wanted to repay Karma for all that it had done for my family and pass it on!

"That would be really nice, daddy," Sharon said. "Thank you! I'll let him know."

I had no idea what would happen, but this was an opportunity to see Richard with family and see if he acted differently.

The Monster's Lap

CHAPTER 3

The Family

❖

Carla and I have never been socialites. We'd preferred to stay at home with the immediate family, and we're not even very comfortable entertaining others at our house, so this particular day was not the most anticipated. I hadn't slept well the night before, so the morning seemed to be dragging on. I loved cooking, though, and I stayed busy in the kitchen roasting the turkey and the many side dishes. I had heard from both Sharon and Richard that Bertran had diabetes, so I contacted a few friends who had diabetes and asked what things I should watch for as far as preparing a Thanksgiving meal. It wasn't until a little later in the morning that Sharon told me she was mistaken and that Bertran didn't have diabetes.

"Bertran recently had some major issues that caused him to go to the hospital, and while he was there, something was said about him having diabetes," Sharon said apologetically over the phone, "but then Richard told me that his dad didn't have it. I'm sorry, Daddy."

"It's fine," I told her. "We still have a wonderful meal that's probably a little healthier for us! Are you on your way?"

"Yeah," Sharon replied. "We'll be there in a few minutes."

True to their word, Sharon and Richard arrived in front of the house a few minutes later, their warm smiles and friendly greetings instantly making them a part of our family gathering.

Although Bertran and I were friends on Facebook, I had never met him before today, and I was surprised at how young he looked. With Richard's help, he made his way to the front door while I looked on. I opened the door and stepped out with as big a smile as possible.

"Bertran!" I said, feeling as if I were greeting an old friend. "It's nice to finally meet you in person. Come in!"

Bertran looked at me and smiled, returning the enthusiasm. He came in and made himself at home. I was just about finished making dinner and setting the table for the feast. Every now and again, someone from the family or guests would wander into the kitchen with praise for how the meal looked or how it smelled. I've always been proud of my cooking skills and love that I can cook with the instinct to cook well.

Once the table was set, there was a quick but thankful prayer, and everyone attacked the food.

The conversation was lively. Carla and I have never been big into sports or politics. Sharon had told Bertran that those subjects shouldn't be approached, especially football, since my mom was in attendance. She had some pretty strong views on her favorite team. Bertran, however, started talking about football nonetheless and was very good at turning the topic toward what would make Mom happy. I had to admit that I was impressed. Richard and his father were very good at making people comfortable around them and were both very likable. I liked Bertran and Richard, and I felt this might be a good family if I could overcome my nagging negative feelings about Richard. I still couldn't quite place what it was.

After dinner, I took Mom home and returned to the house to start the clean-up. While cleaning up, Bertran came in to talk.

"I don't know if you're aware," he started, "but Richard had a pretty rough childhood."

"I haven't heard about his childhood at all," I replied. "What happened?"

"Well, my parents were not very nice people, and there was a point in time when Richard had to go live with them. It was when he was thirteen. He was strong-willed, and after putting up with my parents for a while, he ran away. He lived on the streets for three years."

"Wow," I said, stopping what I was doing. "Why didn't you take Richard in? You're his father."

"Well," Bertran said, somewhat embarrassed, "I was struggling with some issues of my own. I was a slave to drugs. It took me a long time to break it, and I regret that time of my life very much and wish that I could do it differently, but what happened, happened and can't be changed. I just wanted you to know that Richard survived those times. He can look out for himself. He's smart and knows how to care for himself and his family."

"I had no idea," I said, "and thank you for sharing that with me. I'm so sorry to hear that you and he had to endure tough times, but I'm glad you both overcame your challenges!"

Bertran just smiled and walked out of the kitchen. He had said what he needed to say without saying anything further.

As everyone was preparing to leave, we gathered at the front door, and I glanced over at Richard, who was holding two-year-old Julie. There was something about the way he was holding her. It was apparent that Richard loved her, but it seemed that he loved her too much. No, that wasn't it. Something felt wrong, though, about how he interacted with her. I certainly didn't want my imagination to run in directions it shouldn't. Still, something felt more wrong than ever, and now I could put a name to my feelings. Suspicion.

When everyone went home, Carla and I had the chance to sit and talk. I was the first to bring up my feelings earlier in the day.

"Carla," I started, "did you notice anything strange about Richard and Julie today?"

"I didn't notice anything strange," Carla said, "but I had some unsettling feelings."

"Oh?" I said, "Like what?"

"I don't know. There was just something that felt wrong. Something about the way that Richard was interacting with Julie didn't feel right."

"I felt that too," I said. "Something about the way Richard was holding her."

"I felt that too," Carla said, turning towards me. "Something's not right. Something's going on, and it's not good, but I'm not sure what to do." Our shared concern united us in our determination to uncover the truth.

"We can't just accuse him of something unless we know for sure that something is going on," I said. "Besides, if something bad was happening, wouldn't you think Sharon would know? I'm sure she would tell us and wouldn't let it continue."

"I hope that would be the case," Carla said, worried that perhaps her daughter would love this man so much that he would come first in the relationship, even over her own daughter. We both hoped that this wasn't what was going on.

Christmas was just around the corner, and even though we didn't have the money or time to go out, we kept busy. Carla had her full-time job to go to each day, and I kept my home-based business running and took care of transportation for the kids. Things started to get tough when both of our cars broke down on the same day. Carla's car was deemed unfixable for a reasonable amount, and my car, over twenty years old, had a transmission failure. Fortunately, Sharon could help with rides between work and school.

Richard was trying to get his own home business going since he had trouble finding a job with his criminal record. He was still living with Sharon and helping to watch Julie when Sharon was working at night. Richard decided to begin selling things through eBay to make money. Although he could get the account going, he was breaking even. Bertran was able to help out some with a new laptop, printer, and some funds to get the supplies that Richard needed, but Richard maintained that it was going to take time and that he needed to build up his reputation on eBay before things would really take off.

I offered to help by providing Richard with some vintage comic books.

"Any of these that you sell through your account, you and Sharon can keep half of the money," I told him, giving him a few of the comics that were worth the most.

I checked with Richard today to see how things were going.

"I need to find someplace that can give me the values of these before I can list them," Richard said.

"There are several places you can contact online," I told him, "and if nothing else, there are a few comic book stores in town that could probably give you some estimates."

Nothing ever came from the comics, and I wondered if Richard was interested in selling them. I also had an old Commodore Computer system in perfect condition, with a printer and floppy disks with programming. I also offered to let Richard sell that, thinking it would bring a good amount of money. Richard never got around to listing it, so I just kept it safe in his garage. I still have it, and I've realized since then that it's not worth as much as I had imagined. I think it's worth more in sentimental value than it is monetarily.

A few weeks later, Sharon and Richard started visiting often, as I was fond of making cookie trays to give to our friends for Christmas. Richard began hanging out in the kitchen without Sharon, and I had this sinking feeling that Richard was about to have the talk that most fathers dread. Turns out that I was right.

When we were alone, Richard timidly asked, "Can I talk to you briefly about Sharon?"

I remember letting out a large and audible sigh. "Sure. What's up?"

"I want to get your permission to marry your daughter," Richard said, taking out a ring to show me.

"Richard, I like you. If you marry my daughter, you have to promise me that you'll take care of her and Julie and protect them. You have to promise me that you'll find a good job and ensure their futures are secure, and you have to promise me that you'll never hurt them. In the end, however, it's up to Sharon."

"I promise all of that. I want to ask her on Christmas Eve. Thank you, sir," Richard said.

The next day, Sharon came by the house. She asked me if Richard had spoken to me.

"Yeah," I said. "You already knew?"

"He's not very good at keeping secrets, and I heard from a few friends that he wants to ask me," Sharon said. "What did you tell him?"

I recounted the conversation with Richard from the night before, and Sharon nodded. I resisted the temptation to ask Sharon what she was going to do and decided to wait until Christmas morning.

So, Christmas morning came, and I certainly didn't have to ask Sharon or anyone else her answer. Richard was sullen when the family came over, and Bertran didn't say much.

Later on, Sharon spoke with me. "I said that I didn't think it was a good time and that we needed to get to know each other better first. We needed to be more financially secure."

I was very proud of her for having such a level head about this. I wasn't sure what to think about Richard and Bertran's reactions, so I decided to change the subject for now.

"Did you enjoy the cookie tray I brought over? I used a different recipe for the fudge this year."

Sharon fidgeted. "I didn't get any."

"What? Why not?"

"Well," Sharon hesitated, "Bertran and Richard ate all of the fudge, the brownies, and most of the cookies before I was able to get any. I saved a few for Julie, though."

I was furious. How dare they take Christmas treats from my child and my Grandchild? I walked over to a tray on the table, took out two pieces of fudge, and then returned and handed them to Sharon.

"Here," I said. "Enjoy. I'll make more later and ensure you and Julie get them."

Sharon smiled and gave me a big hug. "Thank you, daddy."

"Anything for my little girl," I said, returning the hug.

I wondered if this type of selfishness existed with something as small as confections, what else would they do for themselves?

CHAPTER 4

Custody

❖

The next few months were uneventful. Life seemed to return to a more normal gait. Kids went to school. Parents went to work. Richard continued to work from home but also looked for steady employment. He finally found work as a flagger for a construction company. The hours were long, but at least he brought in some money. Even though he was making some good money, they never seemed to have any extra, and I had to wonder about that. Sharon explained that Richard had numerous bills he was trying to pay off, and the money wasn't there. That always seemed to be the case, and that, in itself, made me uncomfortable. My mind went back to the cookie trays. Did Richard really have as many bills as he claimed, or was he using his money selfishly? I felt terrible for feeling so suspicious, but suspicions in connection with Richard were popping up in my head more often lately. This was not the family I had known, and it was disheartening to see them in such a situation.

Sharon, my daughter, continued working her evening job, and Richard, her partner, watched Julie, their daughter, until Sharon came home at night. Still, by that time, Julie was already in bed and asleep.

In April, Julie turned three. We had a wonderful birthday celebration at our house where the cake was eaten, and gifts were given. It was a fun time.

A few days after that, I was on Facebook and saw a disturbing post by Bertran. It announced how happy he was that Sharon and Richard would be married in June. I called Sharon to ask about this development.

"I saw on Facebook that you and Richard have decided to tie the knot?" I said.

"Um, yeah, I was about to call you," Sharon said. "Who posted that?"

"Bertran posted a very excited post about how he was going to have a daughter-in-law," I said.

Sharon was quiet.

"So you guys are getting married in June?" I asked.

"Daddy, Richard wasn't supposed to tell anyone until we talked to you," Sharon said.

"It's fine, sweetheart," I replied. "We had to find out sometime. I would have rather heard it from you, but that's past. So, June? That's awfully close."

"I don't want to get married in June because of how soon it is," Sharon said, "but Bertran is moving out of the country to marry a girl he met over the Internet. She lives in another country, and he'll be leaving in July. He wants to be at the wedding."

"When did you want the wedding to be?" I asked.

"Maybe August. I don't know. I want it to be a nice wedding where I can have my friends attend and wear my wedding dress. I don't want to get married by a Justice of the Peace."

"Well," I started, trying to put my brain into overdrive, "let's see what happens. Stick to your guns, and we'll figure something out."

I told Carla, and she was upset. She didn't think this was a good idea, and honestly, I didn't either.

Sharon had also been complaining about feeling sick a lot. Carla feared that this was a repeat of what had happened three years earlier and continued to ask Sharon if she could be pregnant.

Sharon had started taking classes to work in medicine and had access to pregnancy tests. She had taken several, and all came up negative. All that is, except for the last one.

Carla came home after speaking with Sharon and broke the news to me.

"I talked to Sharon today," Carla said.

"How's she doing? Is she feeling any better?"

"Not really," Carla said. "She's still pretty sick to her stomach. She'll be going to the doctor's later this week."

"That's good," I said. "Maybe she can figure out what's wrong."

"I think she has already figured it out," Carla said. "She took another pregnancy test, and this time, it came back positive. She's been having morning sickness."

Both of us were quiet for a long time after that. We both knew that Sharon and Richard's future together would probably be set in stone, and we decided that perhaps it was time to be happy for them and hope for the best. Little did we know that fate was ready to step in and change not only Sharon and Richard's lives but also the lives of Sharon's family, a change that would turn all of their worlds upside down. Yet, in the midst of uncertainty, we held onto the hope for a bright future for our family.

Over the next few weeks, Bertran called me almost daily. He was upset that Sharon wanted to delay the wedding and insisted that the couple get married early in the spring before he left. I would sigh and tell him that it was their decision and he would need to respect whatever they wanted to do. As fate would have it, the girl that Bertran was going to marry had developed a brain tumor, and all communications with her and her family ended. Bertran had no way to go to where she was, as her family would pay for him to come over. He was devastated and continued his attempt to reach her, but the new wedding plans would work out just fine in the meantime.

Mid-May arrived, and I had to go out during the evening for my business. Whenever I was working, I always put my phone on silent so as not to be disturbed. Tonight was no different. I had no idea, however, what events were going on across town as I worked. Yet, little did I know, the stage was being set for a series of events that would change the lives of my family and me for a very long time. The anticipation for what was to come was palpable.

Across town, at Sharon's apartment, Sharon was visiting her next-door neighbor. Julie was playing with friends, and Sharon was anticipating a wonderful evening and dinner with her friend. The two women went in and out of the apartment on the warm evening. They were surprised to see two uniformed police officers and a woman dressed in business-like attire walking up the street. It was evident that they were looking for something, and Sharon and her friend were joking about who might be in trouble now. So it took them completely by surprise when the officers turned up the walkway and walked up to Sharon, their expressions serious and their purpose unclear.

One of the police officers spoke up. "Are you Sharon Bolton?" the woman asked.

"Yes," Sharon replied nervously. "Can I help you?"

"Is Richard Pantane your boyfriend? Is he here? We need to speak with him about his registry status."

"Um, yeah," Sharon replied. "He's up in the bathroom right now, but I'll let him know you're here."

Sharon turned to go into her apartment and was about to run up the stairs when the officer asked, "Do you mind if we step in for a moment?"

"Not at all," Sharon said and invited them in.

The officers stood next to the doorway while Sharon trotted up the stairs. She knocked quietly at the door.

"Yeah?" came Richard's voice from the other side.

"Um, the police are here to check with you about your registry status," Sharon said.

"O....kay," Richard said. "I'll be down as soon as I can."

"They're waiting in the house, so if you could hurry, that would be great."

Sharon went back downstairs. "He'll be right down," she told the officers.

When Richard came down, his look was mixed with concern and whimsy. "Hi," Richard said. Can I help you?"

"Mr. Pantane," the male officer said, "I'm Officer Sorenson. Would you mind stepping outside with me for a moment to talk?"

"Um, sure," Richard said and went outside with the officer.

The female officer asked, "Is Julie at home?"

"Yes," Sharon said, "well, she's next door playing. We were going to have dinner with our neighbor."

"Does Richard live here with you?" the officer asked.

"He comes over to shower and sometimes stays the night," Sharon said.

"Could we please see where Julie sleeps? We want to make sure that she's in a safe environment."

Sharon was suspicious that something was up but had no idea what it might be. "Julie," she said, "come upstairs with Mommy for a minute, and let's show my friends your room. They would like to see your princess bed and your toys."

"Okay, Mommy," Julie said, and they went up the staircase. The officer, Julie, and Sharon walked into Julie's room. The woman in business attire followed. Julie started talking about her toys, bed, and which princess she liked best. The officer was very amused and interacted with the little girl. Sharon noticed that the woman in the business suit would vanish occasionally, and she assumed that it was because she was checking out Sharon's bedroom. When she came back, she smiled at Sharon.

"My name is Vivian Campbell. I'm with the Department of Human Services. This is Officer Nelson with Child Protection. Sharon, some allegations have been made that Julie is in a bad situation. Are you aware of anything that Richard might be doing to your daughter?"

Shocked, Sharon immediately answered, "No! He wouldn't do anything to her."

"Sharon, we'll be removing Julie from your home tonight. Are there some family members with whom she can stay?"

Sharon was in shock. She didn't know what to do. "Um, the only family that could take her would be my parents," Sharon said.

"Is there anyone else if they can't take her?"

"No. I don't have any other family close. My parents live just down the street," Sharon said. "I'm sure that they'll take her."

"Please provide me with the names and birthdates of each person living in their house so that I can run a quick background check and ensure that Julie can be there and be safe."

So, all of that was going on while I was working. I had just finished with my client and was almost done loading my equipment into the car. It was about 7:30. I climbed into the driver's seat, took out my phone, and took it off silent mode, noticing that I had several texts and a missed call from Carla. I opened the texts and immediately became concerned. Carla would never text me so many times unless there was something wrong. The first one read, "Family emergency. Please call as soon as you get this!" The next read, "Really need you to call right away!" I was panicked since we still only had one car, and I was afraid that something had happened to one of the kids at home. Without a vehicle, Carla was stranded. I pressed the button to call home, started the car, and began driving. Carla answered right away.

"What's going on?" I asked.

"The police called," she said, out of breath. "They said that they're taking Julie away from Sharon and want to bring her here. Child Protective Services are there and will be here soon. You need to come home!"

"Taking Julie? Why? What happened?" By this time, I was already driving and knew it would take me twenty minutes to arrive home.

"I don't know," Carla said. "They said that they couldn't tell me. They just wanted to know if we would be willing to take Julie for a few days and said neither Sharon nor Richard could contact her. I'll talk with you more when you get here."

My stomach sank. My mind reeled. I was filled with fear and guilt. Why couldn't I have taken action on what I felt earlier before it came to this?

I carefully rushed home. When I arrived, things seemed normal, except for Carla's best friend being at the house. They didn't get to see each other much, and it was rare for her to show up. This time, she was there for support. I said hello, gave her a hug, and then walked over to Carla.

"So what in the world is going on?" I asked.

"Sharon called me and said that the police had arrived at her house. They took Richard outside and spoke with him while a Child Protective Services woman came in with a female police officer. After looking around for a little bit, they told Sharon that they were removing Julie from the home for Julie's own protection. They asked if there was anyone that she could stay with, a family member. Sharon told them that we were the only family she had locally, and they asked her if we would be willing to take Julie for a few days. Then, the social worker got on the phone and asked for the names of everyone living in our house to do a quick background check. They should be here soon." Carla was distraught. We both wondered if Julie was okay and waited as the minutes slowly ticked by with no further word.

I kept checking out the front door to see if anyone had arrived, and eventually, two cars pulled up in front of the house. One was a police car. I took a deep breath and stepped out onto the porch. The police officers were unloading what looked like needed supplies for a little girl's sleepover. They took out a temporary cot, a bag with clothes, stuffed animals, and Julie's favorite blanket. Julie emerged from the other car with a woman who brought up a car seat.

Julie talked excitedly and didn't seem concerned about what was happening.

I smiled as Julie looked up and saw me. "Grandpa!" she squealed and ran to me, jumping into my arms. I picked her up, and she gave me a big, tight hug around the neck.

"I don't think that there's an issue here," the male police officer said, smiling.

I invited the officers in and instructed them to put her belongings on the living room floor next to the front door.

The woman dressed in business attire stepped in and stuck out her hand. "My name is Vivian. I'm with the Department of Human Services," she said. "Thank you for being willing to take Julie. In about ninety percent of these cases, we have to place the child in foster care since there aren't any family members willing or able to take them."

"Of course," I said. "We love our family and would do anything necessary." I started to ask a question, but Vivian cut me off.

"I'll need to inspect your home and see where Julie will be sleeping," she said.

"She'll be sleeping in my youngest daughter's room. I'll show you where it is," I said and led her upstairs for a tour. Carla had already explained what she could to their thirteen-year-old, Kaylie, and asked if it would be okay to have Julie spend a few nights in her room. Kaylie was excited and readily agreed. She and Julie got along really well, and it would be a fun time.

Carla took business cards from the police officers and asked if they could say what was happening.

"We're very sorry, Mrs. Bolton," the female officer stated, "but we can't say anything. You'll have a chance to talk with Vivian in a little bit. Please feel free to contact either of us during the investigation."

"Investigation?" Carla asked, wondering what was being investigated. She worried about Sharon and Julie. She looked at the little girl, who was still excited and running around. She didn't look hurt or concerned. In fact, she seemed normal in every way.

When Kaylie came down the stairs, Julie ran to her. "Auntie!" she shouted and ran to meet her at the bottom of the stairs. "I get to have a sleepover with you!"

"I know," Kaylie smiled, "I heard. I'm excited about that."

"Me too!" Julie said.

"I'll take her cot upstairs in a bit, Kaylie," I said with a weak smile as I descended the stairs. "Right now, could you and Julie go and check out your room? Your mom and I need to talk with the case worker."

"Okay, Dad," Kaylie said. "Come on, Julie. Let's play in my room and let grandpa and grandma talk."

"Okay!" Julie said excitedly, and the two ran up the stairs and out of sight.

"If you don't need us for anything else, we're going to take off," the male police officer told Vivian.

"I don't think so right now," Vivian said. "I just need to talk with Carla and Stephen.

The officer nodded and opened the door, and the two left the house.

"Let's go downstairs into the family room," I said, motioning down the next flight of stairs, "and we can talk there."

The three descended the short flight of stairs and sat down. Vivian sat on one couch while Carla and I sat across from her. There was silence, and no one quite knew what to say, so Vivian took the lead.

"There are a few things that will need to be done right away," she started. "I'm sorry if this upsets your daily routine, but certain procedures need to be followed. Julie will need to see one of our doctors as soon as possible to be checked out. We have a list of doctors that she can go to. She will need to go someplace else either tomorrow or on Friday. You'll need to take her to Safe Kids for a forensic interview. You should not ask her any questions while she's here."

Carla's heart sank, and it showed on her face. She knew what this was all about. I knew as well. Memories of ten years ago came flooding back.

It was like déjà vu. Ten years ago, a family member had sexually molested our daughter, Kaylie. Carla called the police and things took a similar course; doctor's exam and forensic interview. Things were not looking better, but instead, they were looking scary.

"It sounds all too familiar," Carla said. "We went through this before with Kaylie."

"I saw that when I did the background check," Vivian said.

"So, what can you tell us about what's happening?" I asked.

"I really can't talk about it," Vivian said, looking down at her lap. "I can only tell you that some allegations have been made."

"Allegations made by who?" Carla asked, "And against whom? Is Sharon involved in this? I can't believe that she would ever do anything to hurt Julie."

"Again, I can't tell you who made the allegations and whom they are against, but at this point in the investigation, neither Sharon nor Richard are to have any contact with Julie. They cannot see her or talk by phone and are not allowed to come over. If they attempt to do so, you must call the police immediately. Julie is now in the custody of Child Protective Services. Eventually, there will be several court hearings that you will need to attend, and Julie will be assigned an attorney or guardian ad Litem. I'm sure her attorney will contact you. Oh, and there will be a court custody hearing tomorrow. It would be good if at least one of you could be there."

I looked at Carla and then looked back at Vivian. At this point, I would do anything for that innocent little girl upstairs. "At least one of us will be there," he said.

"I've already called my boss at work," Carla said. "She told me to take the day off and do whatever needs to be done and that it can extend for a few days if I need to be here."

"That's great!" Vivian stood and gathered her papers. "I really wish that there was more that I could tell you, but I'm not even going to continue being a part of this case. I do the night and weekend cases, so you will be assigned another case worker who will be in touch with you soon."

Carla and I nodded and escorted her to the front door. As she walked out, she turned and said, "I'm sure this will all be taken care of in the next few days, two weeks tops. Thank you again for being such a caring family."

I closed the door and looked at Carla.

"It's great that they're being so understanding about this at work and that I'll be able to help get things taken care of," Carla sighed. "I'll probably need to take Julie to the doctor's office, but first, we'll need to take her to Safe Child for the interview."

"I can't believe we're going through this again," I said. "At least we know what to expect, but no family should ever have to go through the sexual assault of a child once in their lifetime, let alone twice." I was tired and cranky. I needed to get some sleep.

"Let's go check to see how Julie is doing," Carla said and started up the stairs. I grabbed the cot, pillow, and blankets and followed her up. When we arrived at Kaylie's room, Julie was talking a mile a minute. Carla told Julie to come with her so that she could find a small toothbrush and get her ready for bed. No matter how tired and cranky I get, watching the excitement of a little child makes it all melt away. Every feeling inside is turned to joy.

I started getting the cot ready while Kaylie watched.

"So, what's going on?" Kaylie whispered.

"I'm not sure," I answered and continued to work on the cot. "All we've been told is that some allegations have been made, but we don't know who made them or who they're against."

"What are the allegations?" Kaylie asked. "Did Sharon do something?" Kaylie looked extremely concerned and couldn't believe that her big sister would do anything to hurt Julie.

I stopped working on the cot and smiled at Kaylie. "I don't think that there are any allegations against Sharon, but I don't know for sure. I know we'll have Julie for a few days, but Sharon and Richard aren't allowed to talk with her. Thank you for volunteering to share your room with her, Kaylie. I think it will help her to feel much more at ease."

"Oh, I don't mind," Kaylie said, "and it's only for a few nights."

Carla and Julie came back into the room. Julie climbed onto her small cot and under the blankets. 'Goodnights' were exchanged, and the light was turned out. Carla and I went to our bedroom and got ready for bed, but neither of us could sleep, so we just decided to talk for a while.

"I'll need to call the daycare tomorrow and let them know what's going on," I said.

"I wonder if the daycare knows?" Carla wondered out loud. "Maybe it was the daycare that said something."

"It could be," I said, realizing that my eyes were getting tired now. "I guess we'll find out."

I turned over and kissed the love of my life and the mother of our children. "Goodnight, sweetheart. We'll get this all figured out in the morning."

"Goodnight," Carla said. "I love you."

"I love you too," I returned, and we both fell into a restless sleep, not knowing how much the next few days would destroy our faith in humanity.

CHAPTER 5

The Reveal

❖

The next day, I dropped my kids off at school and stopped by the daycare afterward. I went in and spoke with the administrator after dropping Julie off. Julie was excited to be there and told everyone that her grandpa dropped her off. I kissed her, hugged her, and told her I would be back later to pick her up. Julie smiled and went off to play with her friends. My heart was breaking. I still didn't know what happened, but it was bad enough for the law to get involved.

"My wife and I will be watching Julie for a while," I told the administrator.

"We were informed," the administrator said. "We were also told that Sharon and Richard are not allowed to pick her up or come to see her. Is that correct?"

"That's my understanding as well," I said. "Julie will be going to the doctor's later for an exam. Tomorrow, we have to take her to get a forensic interview. This whole thing is such a mess."

"I'm glad it came out," the administrator said quietly. "The police were here a few times asking questions. I figured that it was a matter of time. Please let me know how things go and if there is anything we can do to help." Her words, filled with genuine concern, reassured me that we were not alone in this.

"Thank you," I said and returned home to pick up Carla for court.

We arrived at the courthouse, went through the metal detector, and then climbed the stairs to the courtroom. When we walked in, the site was slightly confusing. The attorneys who were present were talking and smiling. Sharon and Richard were there. One young female attorney indicated that we should sit next to her. She introduced herself as Jill, Julie's Guardian Ad Litem or GAL, a court-appointed advocate for children in legal proceedings. In front of her was a cake in a box.

When the Magistrate walked in, everyone stood and then sat at her instruction. She asked everyone to identify themselves and then proceeded to talk about why they were there, but not before addressing the presence of the cake box sitting in front of Jill.

"There is a clerk in another courtroom. It's her birthday today, and I was going to bring this to her after this hearing, your honor," Jill said.

"Okay, but I really think that if this hearing takes a little longer, you might want to consider sharing the cake with everyone here," the Magistrate said smiling.

At first, I was shocked at how nonchalant everyone was, but then I realized that these people were just that. They were people. They had lives and families, and in addition to that, they saw the worst things daily that a person could see. They were living, breathing people who had a job to do, and their job was to help others. I couldn't imagine having to go into a courtroom, day after day, and then go home to my family and be cheerful and supportive. Sometimes, I would not even be able to talk about how my day went. I actually felt much better knowing that there were real people who cared, taking care of this and my granddaughter's legal needs and rights. I could have hoped for nothing better.

The Magistrate proceeded to talk about the fact that some allegations have been made and that temporary custody currently lies with the Department of Human Services. She addressed Carla and me, asking if we were willing to assume custody of Julie temporarily. We didn't hesitate to say yes.

The Magistrate told Sharon and Richard that they should get attorneys and that the court could appoint one for each of them if needed. They both indicated it would be good if the court could appoint attorneys. Then the Magistrate noted that Larry, Julie's biological father, would need to be contacted and told about the hearing and the custody situation. Carla and I were completely taken aback and shocked by this statement. Larry hadn't seen his daughter in over a year, but the Magistrate explained that he still had parental rights and had the right to be present if he so desired. At this particular time, however, Larry was in jail and couldn't attend. Hence, the court-appointed an attorney to keep him updated on what was happening. Carla and I were told we didn't need an attorney and were designated Special Respondents in the case. I wasn't sure what that meant, but in the presence of so many attorneys, I felt stupid at the thought of raising my hand and asking.

At that point, the Magistrate indicated that a follow-up hearing would be held at the end of June to assess the situation.

This statement made Carla and me both realize that "two weeks tops" was not going to be set in stone. It now appeared that custody and the "sleep-over" were going to last longer than anticipated. Carla and I looked at this as a time to really get to know our granddaughter and enjoy her company.

As we were leaving the courtroom, Jill approached us.

"Here's my card. Please let me know if you have any questions. You can call or email me anytime. I want to schedule a time to visit you at your home and see Julie in her environment there. Can we schedule that now, or do you need to look at your calendar?" Jill was charming and rather soft-spoken. I couldn't help but wonder if she ever became enraged or passionate about her work. I would find out as time went on.

"I have my calendar on my phone," I said. We can set up a time now, and you're always welcome to stop by at any time to see how things are going."

A home visit was arranged for May 27 at 9 a.m. I was looking forward to this visit, as it would allow Jill to see Julie in her familiar environment, her current attitude, and her emotional state.

As Carla and I returned to the car, we realized that the legal system anticipated the investigation would take longer than we were told. We wondered how much investigating would be done and what would be found. The uncertainty and Julie's prolonged separation from her mother was taking a toll on us emotionally.

After court, Sharon received a phone call from the Police Station. A detective, Cheryl, politely asked if Sharon could come to the station to answer a few questions. Sharon agreed. Richard volunteered to drive her, but Sharon said she would drive herself. Richard decided to meet her there and wait in the parking lot to see what happened.

Looking back, I realize that Richard was nervous about what would happen that day, so he was insistent about being in the parking lot to learn immediately what the interview was all about and the results. He had to hear as soon as possible. That makes me chuckle a little. Keep reading, and you'll see why.

Sharon went into the police station, received a visitor's badge, and followed the desk officer's instructions on how to get to the interview room. Sharon waited in the anteroom until a side door opened, and Cheryl stepped out.

"Hi, Sharon. I'm Cheryl, a Detective here. I've been assigned to investigate this case. Thank you for coming down. Please come in and make yourself comfortable."

Sharon walked in and sat on a loveseat in the small interview room. Cheryl closed the door, sat down, took out a paper pad, and placed a recorder on a table. She indicated the interview would be recorded both through video and audio. The interview started.

Cheryl asked, "Are you aware of the accusations against Richard, and have you seen any difference in Julie since he's been living with you?"

"I haven't seen anything different," Sharon said. "Richard would never do anything to hurt Julie. He loves her."

"I'm wondering if you mind calling Richard and asking him a few questions for me. I'd be curious to see if he'd be willing to come in," Cheryl said.

"I can't do that," Sharon replied. "I don't have my cell phone with me, and besides, he's sitting in the parking lot."

Cheryl raised her eyebrows. "He's in the parking lot? Right now? Why is that?"

"He wanted to drive me but said he'd meet me here so I could talk to him right after my interview."

"Do you think you could get him to come up? I'd really like to talk with him," Cheryl was hopeful.

"I'll ask him," Sharon said and stood, leaving the interview room and building to ask Richard.

"Please don't tell him about the accusations or anything you and I have discussed. I would like to hear what he says without him becoming defensive right off the bat."

"Okay," Sharon said. "I don't feel comfortable keeping things from him, but I'll do what you ask."

Richard's reaction to this request would speak volumes.

Sharon left the building and walked into the parking lot to speak with Richard, anxiously waiting in his car.

"Why do they want to talk to me?" Richard asked.

"I'm not sure," Sharon said. "It certainly couldn't hurt, though, and maybe will even clear some things up."

"I guess so," Richard said, getting out of the car to walk with Sharon into the police station.

Richard went into the interview room and sat down. Cheryl sat across from him.

"Richard, have you heard the allegations in this case?" she asked him.

"No," Richard said coldly.

"It's been alleged that you have had inappropriate contact with Julie."

"That's preposterous!" Richard's voice boomed, raising the already high tension in the room. "Who dares accuse me of such a thing? It couldn't have been Julie. She's not the most articulate, being only three. Who would believe a three-year-old anyway?"

"So you're denying that you've touched her inappropriately?"

"I would never do anything to hurt her!" Richard was outraged.

"Maybe you didn't think you were hurting her," Cheryl said.

"You're trying to coax a confession out of me, but I'm telling you, I'm innocent," Richard retorted, his voice strained.

"Would you be willing to take a lie detector test to verify that?" Cheryl asked.

Richard was quiet and almost froze at the question. "Um, no," Richard said, toning down a little. "I have major anxiety attacks and seizures, so I wouldn't be able to take one. I wouldn't do well with it."

"Maybe you wouldn't do well with it because you're hiding something," Cheryl said. "I'm sure if you tell the truth, everything will go much easier for you."

"Maybe I need to get a lawyer," Richard said.

"If you feel the need for legal counsel, then by all means, seek it," Cheryl said, her tone final. "I have no further questions for you."

Cheryl walked Richard out of the room to the elevator and watched as the doors closed.

Both Carla and I took Julie to Safe Kids.

Safe Kids was a quiet and unremarkable house on the outskirts of town. It had a small parking lot and a nicely kept yard. The house was old but very well maintained. We were familiar with it as this was where we had to bring Kaylie ten years earlier. In ten years, it hadn't changed.

We approached the front door and read the sign hanging next to it: "Please ring the bell for service." I swear that it was the same sign that was there 10 years ago. Wouldn't it have been nice if there was no need for this organization anymore? Thank goodness they were still here, though! I rang the bell and waited. We could hear footsteps inside, and a smiling woman answered.

"Hi. How can I help you?"

"We're here for a forensic interview for Julie Bolton," Carla said.

"We were told to expect you," the young woman said. "I'm Judy, one of the administrators here at Safe Kids. Come in and make yourselves comfortable."

We were all led to a large, living-room-like area. There were toys and a large couch, and beyond that was a kitchen.

"There are drinks and snacks in the refrigerator," Judy said, pointing toward the kitchen. "Feel free to help yourselves." Then she walked into the kitchen and brought out a large bowl filled with various bags of crackers, cookies, and other snacks. "Help yourself to any of these that you'd like. There's also coffee and tea. Someone will be right down to speak with you about what we'll do with Julie."

In the meantime, Julie was fascinated with the various books and toys in the room. She walked over to the table and looked at the snack-filled bowl there. "Grandpa? Can I have a treat?" she asked.

"Oh, I guess so," I said teasingly. "What kind of snack did you want?"

"Hmmm," Julie said cocking her head slightly and considering the bowl. She reached out and moved one bag to reveal a chocolate cracker treat. She smiled and pointed. "That one. I want that treat!"

I had trouble keeping my laughter inside as I reached out, took the bag, opened it, and handed it to the delighted girl. She ate it with great zeal and, when she had finished, looked as if she had smeared a good amount of it on the areas adjacent to her mouth. Carla, with a gentle smile, went into the kitchen, grabbed a paper towel, got it wet, and brought it out to lovingly clean the smiling little face.

Just as she finished, a man in his mid-twenties, with a friendly smile and a professional air, came into the room. "Hi there," he said, sticking out his hand. "I'm Dan. I'll be conducting the interview today."

He shook our hands with a warm smile and then turned his attention to Julie. He knelt down and smiled at her. "This must be Julie! Goodness, you're a big girl. Did you get a snack?"

"Yeah, I got the chocolate crackers, and they were really, really, really good!" Julie said with a beaming smile, her eyes sparkling with pride.

"That's awesome!" Dan replied. "I was wondering if it would be okay if you and I went upstairs into a room with lots of toys so that I could talk to you for a little bit. Would that be okay?"

"Yeah," Julie said, but then she looked at me to verify. I nodded and smiled reassuringly.

"Before we go up," Dan turned to Carla and me, "I'd like to speak with you for a moment or two to explain what we'll be doing."

"That's fine," I said.

I noticed Judy standing in another doorway. She approached us and said, "Why don't you both come here momentarily? We'll explain what's going to happen. I'd also like for you to meet a few people who are here to help you. While we're in the other room, Mary here will watch Julie. Is that okay?"

"Of course," I said. Carla and I walked through the door.

We walked into a cozy room filled with comfortable chairs and loveseats. The walls were adorned with colorful paintings, and there were toys scattered around, giving the room a playful vibe. There were two women already sitting in chairs in the room. They stood up and shook hands with both Carla and I.

"I'm Maddy," said one of the women. "I will be your case worker for DHS." Maddy handed Carla a card. "Feel free to call me anytime if you have questions. I'll be in charge of your case and will be visiting you in your home from time to time over the next several months."

CHAPTER 6

From Weeks to Months

❖

"We were told that this wasn't going to be permanent and that everything would be resolved in a week or so," I said, smiling.

"We need to see what happens today before any decisions are finalized, but at least you can know that you have someone here in case you have any questions."

The other woman stood and introduced herself. "I'm Cheryl. It's nice to meet you. I'm the detective assigned to this case. If you receive any information that might help us resolve this, please don't hesitate to contact me." She handed me her card.

"If we hear anything, we'll be sure to contact you. However, no one can tell us anything at this point, so I'm not sure what we'll find out," I replied. I was beginning to feel somewhat frustrated. It seemed so many people wanted us to inform them, but no one gave us that courtesy.

We sat down, and Judy said, "Dan will be interviewing Julie and asking her some questions. He's been doing this for a long time and is very good with kids. The interview will be videotaped from two different angles. One angle will show Dan and the other angle will focus on Julie. We have microphones in the room to capture what is said. You're welcome to see the video later if you'd like."

"We were here about ten years ago with our youngest daughter," I said solemnly. "I remember going through this. It seems nothing has changed."

"I'm so sorry you must go through this again with your granddaughter. Please let us know if there is anything we can do."

After the brief talk, we returned to the 'living room' area.

"We'll wait here while you go and talk to Mr. Dan," I told Julie, kneeling down to talk with her. "Just come back down whenever you're ready."

Julie and Dan walked off toward the stairs. We seemed to sit for a long time, waiting and not talking much. I was sure we were both thinking about what might be going on upstairs.

Eventually, Julie came bounding back into the room. I thought that perhaps nothing was said until Judy came back in and asked us to return to the small and comfortable room we had left a few moments earlier. Another worker came down and watched Julie while we were gone.

We stepped back into the room and sat down. The caseworker, the detective, the administrator, and Dan joined us. We sat quietly for a moment, after which Dan spoke up.

"Julie did an excellent job. She was very talkative and very coherent. I asked her about the 'tickle' game she mentioned earlier. She told me it was supposed to be a secret, and 'Daddy' told her not to tell. She said Daddy would get mad at her if she told anyone about it. I told her that Daddy wasn't around right now and I wouldn't tell anyone. She then told me that her daddy would tickle her on her bottom. I asked her where that was, and she pointed to her vaginal area. She said that she didn't like it when he would do that. Then," Dan hesitated, "well, something happened that wasn't supposed to happen. One of our workers was talking with another worker out in the hallway and made a noise. When that happened, Julie leaned over to me and whispered that her daddy was out in the hall and that she shouldn't have told, and he would be mad at her now. At that point, she just completely shut down."

We were all quiet. I looked around and saw that Cheryl was taking notes. Maddy was looking at Dan. Carla was looking angry. I knew that she wasn't angry with Dan. She was furious with Richard. I felt absolutely horrible knowing what was happening now. I also felt tears welling up in my eyes. I had hoped this wouldn't be the answer to the question, "What happened?" and yet it was. My daughter's thirty-year-old boyfriend had apparently sexually abused my innocent little granddaughter.

"I think we just need time with our granddaughter," I said, getting up from the chair. Thank you all for being there for us. We walked out. It was difficult to imagine this little girl saying what she had just said to the interviewer. I picked her up and held her. "Are you ready to go?"

"Yeah. I'm getting tired," Julie said.

We walked to the car and headed home. Neither Carla nor I knew what was in store next.

Between the interview and the following evening, we spoke with Sharon, asking if she knew what was happening. Richard was looking for a new place to live so Sharon wouldn't get in trouble. In the meantime, he was back to staying with friends or in his car. Sharon couldn't believe what she was being told about Richard by the police and social workers and told me there had to be a mistake.

"How could something like that happen in the house without me knowing it?" She asked. I had no answers except that those things went on in my house without my knowledge until Kaylie decided enough was too much and bravely told me what was happening to her by a family member.

However, I was about to be hit with another blow to my emotions.

It was close to bedtime on the third night of Julie's sleepover. When I went in to tell her a goodnight story and give her goodnight tucks, Kaylie stopped me.

"Julie wants to talk to you," she said, "before she goes to sleep."

"Oh? About what?"

"She told me that her daddy tickled her last night."

I turned to Julie, lying in her cot in her little nightgown and Pull-Up overnight diaper. I said, "Your daddy didn't tickle you last night. He wasn't here."

"No," Julie said. "He tickled me before. He would tickle me like this."

Julie immediately pulled up her nightgown with her right hand. She began to rub violently between her legs with her left hand. I was speechless, shocked, and embarrassed.

Then Julie said, "It makes me laugh, and then it makes me cry."

Julie got very sad and stopped what she was doing.

I sat her up in the bed, gave her a hug, and said, "Thank you for telling me that. I love you."

Julie hugged me back. "I love you too."

"Get a good night's sleep now, and I'll see you in the morning."

I kissed Kaylie on the forehead, said goodnight, and walked quickly out of the room. I went into my bedroom, where Carla was getting ready for bed. I climbed onto the bed, and tears began to seep from my eyes.

"What is it?" Carla asked.

I fought through the inability to speak one gets when fighting back the tears and told her what Julie said.

We sat quietly for about half an hour, grieving for the small child in the next room. At three years old, she could express what happened, who had done it, and how she felt about it. Still, could she deal with her feelings? Time will tell.

The next day was a Saturday, and the family had a full day planned. It wasn't until we were getting ready to go that we suddenly realized that we wouldn't be doing many things together for at least the next few weeks. A few months earlier, both of our vehicles broke down simultaneously. The more spacious of the two cars was declared a total loss when the engine had to be replaced at a cost of over four thousand dollars. The smaller economy car died on the same day. Not having much money, we were entirely without a car. A friend of mine came to the rescue by offering to sell me her car as she was preparing to buy a new one. I could make payments whenever I could. It was a great blessing, and of course, I agreed. The car was a Subaru station wagon. A great little car, but it only seated five people. Since we currently had three teenagers at home and now Julie, there was no way we could fit everyone in the car, especially with a car seat! It was going to be a very interesting few weeks. So, if someone volunteered to stay home, the rest could go out. We were used to doing things as a family, and now that wasn't possible. So, we all stayed home, and everyone helped around the house. There were things to do in the yard, and Julie jumped on the trampoline with Kaylie. It ended up being a good day.

As evening rolled around, I had some work on the computer, so Carla went to tuck in the little girl before I could come upstairs. Carla said from the top of the stairs, "The girls are ready for bed if you want to come up and say goodnight."

"Thanks, hun," I replied and did, this time without incident. After saying "goodnight," I went into the bedroom to talk with Carla for a moment. She was distraught.

"What's going on, hun?" I asked.

"Julie wanted to talk to me about 'the tickling' when I went in. What she said and did made me sick."

"I'm afraid to ask," I said. "Was this different than what she told me last night?"

"Yeah. She sat on the edge of her cot and straddled the corner. Then she started thrusting back and forth with her hips. She said, 'Daddy would make me sit on top of him and do this!' then she stopped and was sad. I asked her what was wrong. She told me that she was grumpy. I asked her why she was grumpy, and she said, 'I'm grumpy because I didn't like doing that. It didn't feel good.'"

"Is there a possibility that maybe she saw Richard and Sharon having sex?" I asked.

"I don't think so," Carla said. "She's had her own room for quite some time. Besides, she never says that she saw Daddy doing this to Mommy. It's always, 'This is what he did to me' or 'This is what he made me do,' so I'm pretty sure that's not it."

"I just can't imagine a thirty-year-old man, with a beautiful girlfriend, wanting to do this kind of thing to a three-year-old child. It doesn't make sense to me."

"It doesn't make sense to me either, but then I don't think that way, and neither do you."

"He needs to get some help," I said. "One story was bad enough, but now two different stories?"

I felt sick to my stomach. I couldn't understand why he would do this to a sweet and innocent little girl. I felt like I failed my daughter and my entire family. As a father, I want to fix everything. This was something that I couldn't fix, and it was more than frustrating.

Once again, we both fell into silent sadness. What else could this man have done to this little girl? We didn't want to know. We hadn't asked her to tell us, but she volunteered so much. I figured once she told the interviewer what happened and didn't get in trouble, she felt it was okay to say to others, as long as they wouldn't tell "Daddy."

The next day, I had to run to Wal-Mart and grab a few things. I couldn't get what Julie said out of my mind and kept wondering what I could do or give her to help her get over and through this ordeal. I went to the self-checkout lanes and scanned the few things I had bought. That's when I heard the voice.

"Hey, Stephen. How's it going?"

I froze. I knew the voice, but I didn't want to look up. I had never been confrontational, and I didn't want to start now.

When I finally looked up, there stood Richard. He had grown his hair a little longer since the last time we saw each other. He had a half smile on his face, but his eyes were puppy dog sad.

"Hi Richard," I said coldly, and continued to scan my items.

"I was just here to deposit some money into Sharon's bank account," Richard said, "but I guess I got here too late. They're closed."

"Uh huh." I really didn't feel like talking to Richard, not after everything I had heard from Julie this week. I was angry. I wanted to walk away, but Richard had this way of being friendly and jovial. He made people feel comfortable around him.

"How's Sharon doing with all of this?" Richard asked.

"She's upset. Her daughter has been taken away from her."

"I'll bet," Richard said quietly. "I wish there was some indication as to who would say something like this. We both love Julie and would never do anything to hurt her."

"I know," I said. "I need to get going. Where are you staying?"

"I was staying in my car, but I found a friend that said I could stay with him for a while. It's just a little ways south of here, so it doesn't take me long to get to work."

"That's good," I said. "Hopefully, this whole thing will be resolved soon. Take care, Richard."

I turned and walked off. I couldn't believe that Richard could stand there and talk to me like nothing happened. I could feel that I was shaking. For the first time, I wondered what had really happened and what the truth might end up being. I also knew that I didn't want Richard to be around my daughter or my granddaughter anymore.

When I got home, I told Carla about my encounter. Carla was visibly disgusted. She had formed her opinion about Richard and she wanted to see him go away.

Over the next few weeks, Julie told more stories. She told a total of three to me, three to Carla and three to Kaylie. Each story was different, and each story made the family sad and sick. The saddest part was that it suddenly made Kaylie start feeling the pains of her past abuse. She had forgotten what had happened, and still couldn't remember, but something was there, boiling in her subconscious. So Carla and I decided that it might be time for her to go back into therapy. We still had money on the Victim's Compensation account for just such a time and we decided to use it. Kaylie's old therapist was still in practice and when we contacted her, she was more than willing to help out and set-up an appointment. This whole thing with Julie would be farther-reaching than any of the family could ever imagine!

In the meantime, Carla started having some physical problems. She developed pain in her hands and feet along with pain in her shoulders, neck, abdomen and lower back. Even though she went to the doctor, they were unable to find a cause, so she lived with the pain as best she could with Advil and rest. This one event was beginning to have more consequences on our family than anyone imagined. Our physical, mental, and emotional health was deteriorating, and there was nothing we could do about it.

CHAPTER 7

The Routine

❖

Despite the stress of managing our daily routines, we remained resilient, always putting the needs of our family first. This resilience was a testament to our love and commitment to each other.

Julie settled in well and enjoyed spending time with her aunts, uncles, and grandparents. Every now and again, she asked about her mom, but she never asked where "Daddy" was. Our family, united in our love for Julie, provided her with a stable and nurturing environment.

May 27th arrived and I cleaned the house, drove everyone to their assigned destinations, and then returned home and fixed Julie something to eat. Jill was going to visit today for a home visit. Carla didn't have to be at work until noon, so she was at home to hear what would be said and ask any questions she had. Soon, the doorbell rang. I answered the door and invited Jill inside. Carla, Jill, and I went downstairs, with Jill on one couch and Carla and I on the other by Julie, where we talked while Julie ate and watched some TV.

"How's she doing?" Jill asked. "She looks like she's happy."

"She is," I replied. "She loves staying here and visiting with her aunts and uncle. I don't think she minds visiting with Carla and me either," I laughed.

Julie came over and climbed on my lap.

"I wanted to let you know that if she starts to talk with you, or anyone in the family, about what has happened, it's best not to ask her any questions," Jill said.

That hit me hard. I was quiet for a moment and then spoke up. "She has already been talking to us all. She's told numerous stories. We listen and give her hugs. We don't ask her to expound on anything at this point. I'm not certain we want to hear any more detail than what she's already telling us. She's being precise about things, and it's disturbing."

"Could you write down what she's saying and send it to me in an email? I would like to know what she's saying about what's going on and have a record of it."

"Yeah. That's fine. I can do that. I'll get Kaylie to do the same thing." Carla nodded that she would also write down what she was being told.

"I appreciate it," Jill said. "I know this must be very hard on all of you, but you're doing the best thing for Julie by keeping her safe and watching over her. Has Richard or Sharon tried to see Julie? I want to assure you that we are all here for Julie, and we will do everything we can to support her through this difficult time."

"No," I said. "Sharon has talked with Carla and asked how Julie is doing, but we haven't heard from Richard. Bertran, Richard's dad, calls me often. He seems to be on board with doing whatever is best for Julie. When will we know more about what's going on? Sharon is Julie's biological parent, and Richard is just the boyfriend. We've always had a good relationship with them. We never expected something like this to happen, and it's been a shock for all of us."

"I can tell you that Richard was accused of having inappropriate sexual contact with Julie. DHS wanted to get her out of a potentially bad environment, so she's here. There will be a thorough investigation before Julie can return and live with Sharon, but things are moving quickly. We want to be sure that Julie will be safe."

I thought about what else I wanted to ask. "So, it's almost been two weeks since Julie came to live with us. We're having a great time with her and can see numerous improvements in her behavior, but when she first came over, we were told that it would only be for a few weeks. Do you have any idea how long something like this typically takes?"

"It will depend on the case's complexity," Jill said, "and the final allegations. Then, depending on what the detective finds out, there might be criminal charges."

I was taken aback by this statement. "Criminal charges? Do you mean like jury trial and jail time? Is Sharon looking at facing these charges?"

"Again, I can't say anything until after the police have investigated more, but I'll let you know as soon as possible. I'm sure you and Carla are anxious about what all of this means, but we need to do things according to the law so it's done correctly for Julie's sake."

"You're right, of course," I said, but I couldn't help but worry about what this would mean to Sharon.

"So, will the criminal case be separate from what's happening now?" Carla asked.

"Yes," Jill said. "This is considered a civil case, and the police are not involved in this side of it. Suppose the police, once they've finished the investigation, find enough evidence to show that something happened to Julie. In that case, they will present it to the District Attorney. If he feels the evidence is convincing enough to prosecute, he'll press charges, and a warrant will be issued."

"What does that mean for Julie?" Carla asked. "Would she be required to testify in court?"

"The law states that the accused has the right to confront his accuser," Jill said, "but I'm sure that at her age, there must be ways that we can get her testimony and have it admitted into court without a face-to-face confrontation. I certainly don't want her to be traumatized any more than she already is. This whole thing is about

Julie and keeping her safe from any further harm, whether it's mental or physical. We all need to pull together and make sure that happens. You two are doing a great job with her and I can see that she's safe and happy. That's the important part right now. Just keep doing what you've been doing and email what all she says to you."

After a while of talking, Jill said she needed to get to court and would be in touch soon. She reminded me to send a hard copy of Julie's statements and said that the permanent case worker would contact me soon to set up another meeting at the house and, down the road, a family meeting to discuss what steps would be coming next.

I thanked her and closed the front door. I hadn't really thought about the criminal part of all of this. I wished I knew to what extent, if any, Sharon was involved. On the phone, she said that she didn't know what was going on and what accusations could have been made, but she couldn't think of anything that had been done. In fact, when I shared with her what Julie was saying, she was shocked and sincerely so. She didn't believe that Richard could have done something like this, but at the same time, she had to acknowledge her child's words. The hardest part for Sharon in all of this was that Julie had not said anything to her about what had happened. She didn't understand this until Julie made another disclosure one night to me.

Julie had just told me something else that had happened at Richard's hand, and, as always, I hugged Julie and thanked her for telling me what had happened. Then Julie said something interesting. She said, "Daddy told me I could never tell Mommy about the tickling game."

"Really?" I asked in surprise.

"Yeah," Julie said. "He said that if I told Mommy, it would make her cry."

I was very sure, at that point, that not only did Sharon not have anything to do with the abuse but also that she had no idea that it had happened. She was in love with Richard. How do you convince someone that the person they love is doing unspeakable things to your child? I constantly wished that this had never happened for the sake of so many people under my roof.

Over the next few weeks, Sharon, who had started missing Julie more, moved in with Carla and me after we received permission from Jill. While staying with us, she also maintained her residence. She stayed every night at our house to be close to Julie. Although she wasn't allowed to stay at her apartment alone with Julie, she was able to spend time with her at our house at night under our supervision. It was better than not being able to see her at all.

On May 30th, Sharon took Julie in to see the doctor. The doctor said that everything looked intact and that it didn't appear that any penetration had taken place. Inwardly, Sharon gave a sigh of relief. She went home and called her mom to let her know the news. It was also a relief for Carla to hear, but in a different way than it was for Sharon. Sharon continued to hope that Richard hadn't done anything, as he maintained. This was one piece of good news in his favor.

Carla told me that night what she had learned from Sharon.

"That's good!" I said enthusiastically. "Maybe it's just a big mistake," I said the words, but inside and with everything Julie had said, I didn't believe them.

"That would be nice," Carla said. "I guess we'll find out as the investigation continues. It's hard to believe that Julie would tell us so many stories about what happened to her, pointing to Richard each time and telling us how she felt each and every time something had happened."

"I know what you mean," I said. "Every story is different, and each one tears me up. Kaylie's not doing so well with them, either. It seems like she's been down more and more lately."

As routine as everything became, Carla and I had realized ten years earlier that we were not having any more children. We looked forward to the day when we would become grandparents and could hand the grandchild off to the parent when things became less fun. After all, isn't that what grandparents are entitled to do? They reap the benefits of having fun while leaving the disciplinary tasks to the parents. Now things were reversed. Carla and I had once again assumed the role of parents raising a young child. Although Sharon was staying at the house, she was five months pregnant with Richard's child, and her morning sickness lasted most of the day. So when she wasn't at work, she rested on the couch while Carla, Kaylie, and I watched Julie. It was mostly Kaylie who watched her. They were very close, and, for the most part, it didn't seem like a chore for her. They would play, talk, and paint their nails. Kaylie would put in movies for them to watch and put Julie to bed at night. She did a tremendous amount and helped more than any other thirteen-year-old would have done in her position. Carla and I were very grateful for her help. Our family, despite the challenges, was resilient and strong.

I started making bigger meals to feed both Sharon and Julie. Sharon would help with groceries using her food stamp card. This was done at the suggestion of DHS since Carla and I were watching Julie full-time.

Sharon enjoyed any help she could get with Julie since she wasn't feeling well, but she also missed Richard. She was still trying to reconcile everything in her mind and decide if he had really done anything to hurt Julie. It was a significant conflict of both her mind and her heart. The emotional toll of the situation was evident in her eyes, and it was a constant reminder of the fragile state of our family dynamics.

Legally, things were moving very fast. Interviews, court dates, setting up home visits, attorneys, and an endless number of requests for information. Then, as quickly as it all had started, everything suddenly stopped. It was quiet. The only surety at this point for Carla and I was that we still had custody of Julie. However, there was a family meeting on Carla's and my calendar on June 10th, which was glaringly obvious. Family meetings were not conducted in the home, and Julie would not be present. Family meetings were conducted in a building that combined the forces of law enforcement and DHS. I didn't know what to expect, and Carla and I drove to the location in silence, not even having enough information to speculate about what was coming up.

When we arrived, we had to wait in a lobby area until the DHS caseworker led us through a maze of corridors to a meeting room. I had to wonder why all government offices were set up as a maze in the back areas. It may be to confuse people who were visitors if they tried to escape. I could envision the government workers all standing in the hallways, pointing and laughing at a visitor who was unsuccessfully trying to quickly find their way out. I shook the thought from my head and took Carla's hand as we walked. My heart was pounding, and I couldn't shake off the feeling of uncertainty that hung in the air.

A piece of paper was passed around once we were seated in the meeting room. A gentleman at the front of the room, the moderator, told everyone they needed to sign in with their names, phone numbers, and email addresses. Carla and I already knew most people in the meeting except one person. The young woman was introduced as Courtney and involved in the Kinship Program. She explained that this program is in place to help with the needs of families who have custody of a child who is their relative but doesn't belong to them. Over the next few months, Carla and I found this program very helpful. The support from the Kinship Program was a reassuring presence in our lives. I learned there were some other agencies that had similar programs in place.

In the meeting, they discussed what would happen next with court hearings on the DHS side, how custody needed to work, and how visits between Sharon and Julie would go. The discussions were focused on ensuring Julie's safety and well-being, as well as the measures that needed to be taken to achieve this. Sharon was allowed to stay at our house at night. She was allowed to bring Julie to her apartment during the day, but only with the assurance that Richard would not be there. It was emphasized that there was an order of protection in place and that if Richard showed up at either Sharon's or our home, the police were to be called immediately. All of the rules were reviewed and agreed upon. Our family was determined to protect Julie at all costs, ensuring our home was a secure place for her. Richard was not present at this meeting even though he knew about it. We all discovered that he knew about the meeting when Sharon shared that Richard had synced his phone with Sharon's and could, therefore, see all of Sharon's appointments in addition to her email correspondence.

"This isn't a good thing, Sharon," the DHS caseworker said, concerned. "You need to secure another phone or, at the very least, a new email address."

"I can't afford to get a new phone," Sharon said, her voice tinged with worry. "I'll look into getting a new email address but I honestly don't think Richard will do anything with the information."

As I look back on this horrible time in our lives, I realize how controlling Richard was. He always needed to know what was going on firsthand without having to be confronted by authorities.

Courtney, one of the people in attendance was a petite young woman who was very soft-spoken. After the meeting, she approached Carla and me.

"Before you leave, I must get your fingerprints and personal information. I need to run a background check on both of you," Carla said.

"I thought they already ran a background check on our entire family?" I questioned.

"That was neither a complete nor in-depth check," Courtney said, her dedication to the task evident. She handed both Carla and I sheets of papers. "Please fill out these forms completely with your personal information. If you have any questions, please let me know."

We sat down and answered the fundamental questions about who we are, where we've lived, previous names, etc. I finished mine first and stood up. Courtney came over and took the form.

"Okay, Stephen," she said, "it looks like you've filled everything out. Please come back with me so that I can get your fingerprints."

I followed her back to a large machine. She sprayed my fingers with water and instructed me on how to place my fingers on the glass for scanning.

I've always liked kidding around and making light of things, especially in awkward, first-time situations.

"What happens if you get a bad report about someone's background?" I asked Courtney light-heartedly.

She stopped what she was doing and gave me an icy stare. Then, in an equally cold voice, Courtney asked, "Will I find something bad when this comes back?"

I had been in my share of fights, and there weren't many people I was afraid of. In this case, I couldn't say I was scared of Courtney. Still, at that moment, I respected her authority and whatever power came with that authority. My answer was half joking. "I have no background, so you won't find anything bad. In fact, when I'm in restaurants, the waiters often ignore me because I'm fairly invisible to the public."

Courtney didn't laugh but resumed her work. "That's all I need from you now, Stephen. If your wife is done with her form, please send her back." Her tone returned to normal, and I felt less tense. Still, I wondered what, if anything, the state investigative background check might turn up.

I gathered the courage to ask when Courtney came over with the DHS caseworker for a home visit.

"So, Courtney, did you find anything bad on my background check?"

Courtney squirmed in her seat a little, which made me uncomfortable. The only people there were Carla, Courtney, Julie, and the new DHS caseworker, Lana. "Is it okay to talk openly?" Courtney asked.

"Of course," I said. "There are no secrets here."

Courtney looked down and then spoke. "I found something about your youngest daughter in the background check. Apparently, she was molested when she was younger by a family member. This information is relevant because it could affect Julie's safety in your home."

"Yes," I replied. "That's correct. My son went through all of the necessary treatments and is fine now. My daughter is back in therapy and is working toward remembering what happened and dealing with it. Why is that an issue?"

"Well," Courtney was uncomfortable in her answer, "does he live here or visit at all?"

"He doesn't live here but does visit," I said, "and I have every confidence that he is fine around Julie."

"We would feel better if he were not allowed to be alone with her at this point," Courtney said.

I didn't feel good about her statement, but I understood why she said it. "Well, when he comes over, we are all present. He doesn't stay the night, and I'm sure everything will be fine. It was a long time ago, and I don't feel he is a threat to Julie…at all."

"Still," Courtney said, "it would be best if he weren't alone with her."

I had a feeling at that moment that my son would never be trusted in the eyes of the powers that be because of one mistake, and I wondered how Richard would fare in this particular situation. My son had made it through treatment, and I was proud of the young man he was becoming. I hoped that Richard would opt for treatment and become better than he was, but I wasn't sure that Richard would agree to that. He was totally against any evaluation, tests, or treatment. I felt sad about that.

"We'll make sure that someone is always here when he visits," I said, moving on to another subject.

Over the next several weeks, Carla and I found that the system was on our side. Assistance was given to help pay for Julie's daycare. Clothes were brought over for Julie, and games and toys were brought to help her while she was at our home. This support reassured us and gave us hope during this challenging time.

July came, and the meetings and court hearings continued. We went to court once each month, had a home visit once each month, and had a family meeting once each month.

Richard eventually filled out the paperwork to get a Public Defender and was represented at the hearings. At the beginning of July, there was a court hearing. Everyone anticipated that it would be regarding custody. So it was a surprise when, fifteen minutes after being at the courthouse and just moments before the beginning of court, everyone received a copy of the treatment plan. The treatment plan talked about how Sharon needed parenting classes and therapy. Julie was to receive therapy. Larry had to receive therapy, and Richard had to go through a sexual offense-specific treatment program. When the hearing started, the Magistrate asked if there were any questions regarding the treatment plan and if everyone agreed.

"Your Honor, we all have just received the proposed treatment plans and haven't had time to thoroughly go over them with our clients," Sharon's attorney said.

"My client, Larry, Julie's father, hasn't shown up again, and I'll have to see if I can locate him to go over this with him," Larry's attorney said.

Richard's attorney stood to address the court. "Your honor," he started, "my client will not do the sexual offense-specific treatment listed in the treatment plan since he has not committed a crime."

The Magistrate looked at the attorneys and smiled. "I'll give you all some time to go over these and find out why they were not delivered to you in a timely manner. In the meantime, there has been a motion to expand the order of protection to include no contact between Mr. Pantane and Ms. Bolton and between Mr. Pantane and the Special Respondents, Mr. and Mrs. Bolton."

Richard's attorney again stood. "Your honor, my client objects to the expansion of the protective order. He feels there is no need to limit contact between himself, the Special Respondents, and Ms. Bolton since he has not been accused of doing anything to them."

"Your objection is noted, and we will visit this again in two weeks on July 14. We will adjourn until that time."

Everyone stood as the Magistrate left the room.

Carla and I were totally shocked by this hearing. From what we had heard, this was supposed to be a hearing about when Sharon could get custody back, but custody was never mentioned. We also wondered how changes in the protective order were suggested and how they could be so easily dismissed. It was strange, and we didn't understand the legal system most of the time, including today. We did know that another meeting was scheduled for the fourteenth. They called it a Facilitation. We would soon find out what this meant!

The date came for the Facilitation, and everyone except Larry was there. Richard refused to abide by any of the suggested treatments and denied that any allegations against him were valid.

To get things moving along, Sharon agreed that she had allowed Julie to be in an unsafe environment and also agreed to the treatment plan. She would set up appointments with therapists and the Parenting classes for both her and Julie.

Larry's attorney said he had been trying to reach Larry without success. Hence, the court ordered that Larry get therapy.

Because Richard decided that he had done nothing and refused everything, the court decided to set a jury hearing to decide if, based on the evidence, something had happened to Julie at Richard's hand. This would not be a criminal hearing but to determine if something had happened. There would be Pre-Trial activity from the attorneys to prepare for this trial. The trial was set for September 10th and 11th.

For unknown reasons, over the next few weeks, Richard decided he no longer wanted to be a "Special Respondent." Instead, he wanted to be listed as a "Respondent." It was unclear why he did this because he lost the right to a trial by jury in the D and N (Dependency and Neglect) hearing. In addition, the Magistrate indicated that everyone listed as respondents or special respondents were required to appear at the hearing. Failure to appear would result in a contempt of court charge. Larry's attorney stood to address the court. "Your Honor," he sighed. "I have not been able to locate Larry, and neither have the authorities. I will, however, continue to attempt to find him and request that he attend."

Julie started "play therapy." Sharon and I went to the first session and learned what would be going on during the therapeutic time. I also learned that the therapist could not share any information about anything discovered with either Carla, Sharon, or me due to a new law created from a recent court case. I was disappointed, to say the least. I had hoped to learn more about what was going on with her, but I sincerely didn't want to know any additional stories. It was becoming too painful!

On the other hand, Richard had told Sharon that he didn't want Julie to have any therapy. He was afraid she would be coached to say things, and he was worried that she was also being coached at daycare. He wanted Julie to stay away from both daycare and therapeutic settings. Richard's paranoia was growing and evident to everyone at this point. Still, Sharon told him that this was impossible and continued to take Julie to both.

Around this same time, I was trying to get the old records from the police regarding my youngest daughter's assault ten years earlier. I emailed Cheryl, and she found a case number from those many years ago. With that information, I went in and picked up the records from the police department. I had dreaded this day but knew that it would not only be best for Kaylie to read the statements in a therapeutic setting but that it would be a while before that happened. This was a time that I didn't want to relive but would for my daughter's sake.

July came and went. Carla and I had now been Julie's guardians for two and a half months. The courts started to order action on the treatment plans. Larry, who had admitted to allowing her to be in an unsafe environment, was ordered to take therapy sessions. Likewise, Sharon received the same order and set a time to begin those sessions. She felt it would do her good to talk with someone about parenting and taking care of children. She would soon be a single mother of two children and wanted all the help she could get, a testament to the support system around her.

August 4th brought another trial. I was unable to attend, but Larry was there with a girlfriend. Richard was very upset because the girl Larry was with was his former girlfriend. Irony appears in the strangest places. It's weird to me how these two individuals, Larry and Richard, had never met, yet they had so much in common.

The court was resolute in its decision to see everything move ahead, bolstering our confidence in the legal process.

On August 8th, Cheryl called Sharon down to the police station for another interview. She wanted to see if Sharon had any additional information to add to her previous interview and if any new information had come to light. Sharon couldn't think of anything new to add.

"Do you feel that he might try to run?" Cheryl asked.

"I don't know," Sharon said. "I know that he has friends in Washington State and has indicated that if he went there, he would be exempt from extradition, and even if someone came looking, he could probably hide there for a long time without getting caught."

"That wouldn't be a smart thing to do," Cheryl said, "considering that he can be expedited from Washington State, and then he would have to pay for all expenses for the police to bring him back."

Later that day, I received an email from Cheryl which read:

"…I'm sure that your wife probably told you, but the DA is going to accept the charges. I am actually working on the warrant now. I'll let you know when I learn more, but it's pretty good news!"

I was happy to hear that the DA would take it to trial. I emailed Cheryl back and asked if Sharon knew. She replied:
"…I haven't told Sharon I am working on the warrant because she is still communicating with Richard, and I want him to be surprised by it, and I want to use whatever info he gives to Sharon which may come to a halt when he's arrested."

Carla and I were both relieved and concerned about Sharon. How would she take this? She still felt a strong emotional attachment to Richard and had only seen him a few times since this happened. Her heart was breaking already, and I wondered how much more Sharon's heart could take.

I have to wonder how much my heart can take. It's getting tough, taking so much time, and taking a heavy emotional and mental toll on me.

CHAPTER 8

A New Chapter

❖

As it always seems to do in the summertime, August crept by slowly. A Permanency Planning Hearing was set for September 4th. Sharon was getting bigger and more uncomfortable. She was having trouble with her back and legs. Carla, Kaylie, and I helped out as much as we could.

Despite Carla's condition continuing to worsen and her pain reaching extreme levels on some days, the family remained resilient. The doctors' struggle to find the cause of Carla's pain was discouraging, but the family's strength helped keep Carla strong and focused.

The family's unwavering support for Kaylie was evident as she continued with her therapy to prepare to read her original transcripts and remember what had happened to her. Their commitment to her recovery was a source of reassurance.

Julie's resilience shone through as she received funding from the Kinship Program to take gymnastic classes at daycare. She found immense joy in this, and her enthusiasm was infectious. Her determination to find joy in the midst of adversity was truly inspiring.

At the end of August, Jill requested that Carla and I act as witnesses during the upcoming trial. This trial was crucial in determining Julie's future and holding the responsible parties accountable. She wanted someone to tell the court what Julie had disclosed during her stay.

On August 29th, I opened the mail to find a summary of the current situation with Sharon, Julie, and the others involved with the case. It talked about how Julie's needs were met at our home. Sharon had started all of her treatments. Larry was concerned that Richard and Sharon still had an ongoing relationship. Finally, Richard had contested the treatment plan, which required him to complete a psychosexual evaluation and comply with any recommended treatment. The Department of Human Services, a key player in child welfare at that time, decided that Richard should not have any contact with children until he completed the treatment plan. This would all be addressed in the upcoming court hearing.

Richard and I were still communicating. I wanted to make sure that I knew where he was and what he was thinking. He was still free, and I hoped he wouldn't get spooked and run.

Attorneys would send information to my house for Richard since he had listed our residence as his mailing address, and I would take them to Richard, where he worked. I wanted to make sure Richard was aware of everything going on, and I wanted to ensure I knew he was still in town. Richard was likable. I've since learned that many sociopaths are like that. They can make people believe they are pleasant and that things happen to them, not because of anything they do to invoke these bad things but because of consistent lousy luck. While I believed Julie, I still had trouble believing that he, or any adult, could do what Julie said that he did. Still, how does a three-year-old make something like that up? In one of the stories, she told me, "Daddy would take off my panties and then take off his pants." That thought made me feel uneasy and sick to my stomach. I didn't like to think about it. Maybe that's why no one talks about these things; it makes most of us feel sick and helpless. It's not natural to take advantage of a child this way. Writing about these things and reflecting on what happened is difficult, but I feel it all needs to be told. Maybe it will help others stop something from going on in their family. Perhaps it will make a person think twice before committing such a crime. At the very least, I hope it will help educate a family and assist them in understanding the process of what will come after such a crime is discovered.

Richard became aware that the warrant for his arrest was active and, as anyone might expect, this bothered him. He waited outside of Sharon's workplace one evening to talk with her.

"I'm going to turn myself in," he told her. "I think it would be the best thing to do."

"I think so too, Richard," Sharon said.

"Will you support me in this? Will you stand by me throughout whatever is going to happen? I love you, you know. I want us always to be together. You have to believe that I didn't do anything to Julie, and I never would do anything to hurt her. I love that little girl more than my own life." Richard was almost pleading.

"I will stand by you," Sharon said. "Let me know when you're going to turn yourself in."

"Will you drive me there?" he asked.

"Yeah," Sharon said. "It will be hard, but I'll do that for you."

Richard gave Sharon a hug and then turned to go back to his car. He stopped for a moment and said, "I love you, Sharon."

"I love you too," she replied, but her heart hurt with the conflict that comes from trying to choose between two people that you love.

Carla and I waited to hear that Richard had turned himself in, but word never came. On August 29th, it was the Friday before Labor Day; Sharon came home and talked with me. "So, I guess Richard has left the county."

"Oh?" I said surprised and half not so surprised.

"Yeah," Sharon said. "He went to another city out of the county because he said he had a bad feeling about this weekend."

"I thought that he was going to turn himself in?" I asked.

"I thought so too, but he has things he wants to get done before that happens, so he's putting it off."

"I hope he doesn't wait too long," I said, shaking my head. "It will look much better for him if he turns himself in than if he's arrested."

"I know daddy," Sharon said. "I know."

On September 3, 2014, my phone rang. I looked at the screen and saw that it was Sharon.

"Hello? How's my girl?" I said into the phone.

"I'm alright," Sharon said. "I thought you should know that Richard was arrested a few minutes ago."

"Really? What happened, and how do you know?"

"I got a call from Bertran. It would seem that they were running around town in Richard's car, and he was pulled over," Sharon said nonchalantly.

"So I guess that his 'feeling' was right. Why did Bertran call you?" I was curious since Bertran had been talking to me so often. I assumed he would have called me, but perhaps he didn't want to face that embarrassing moment with me there.

"He was riding as a passenger and doesn't have a license. The police asked if someone could come and get the car, so Bertran called me."

I had a million questions, but I wanted to ask the most important ones first. "So, was he pulled over because of the warrant?"

"Not really. Do you remember I told you how his license plates expired in May? Well, he was pulled over because he was driving with expired plates. He never got them renewed. If he had renewed his registration, he probably wouldn't have been pulled over. When they ran his name, the warrant came up, and they arrested him," Sharon said. "He should have just turned himself in when he said he was going to. It would have looked better for him."

"Yeah," I said. "It's a scary thing looking at what he's looking at. It would take a lot to walk in and let them take you, but you're right. It would have looked better for him. I guess we'll see what happens next."

One word. Karma.

On September 4, Carla, Sharon, and I went to court again. At court, the Magistrate discussed returning Julie to Sharon. Richard was in jail and so wasn't present in court. Larry wasn't there either, but their attorneys represented both. Carla and I were expecting that Julie would possibly be allowed to begin visits to Sharon's apartment now that Richard was in jail. What the Magistrate said came as a shock to us both.

"Although reunification with the family shall remain a part of the case plan in this matter, it is not appropriate that the Child be returned to the Respondent at this time. Reasonable efforts have been made to avoid continued placement out of the home and to finalize the permanency plan. There is a substantial likelihood that the Child will be returned to the physical custody of one or more of the Respondents within six months of today's date. It is anticipated that the permanency goal should be completed by March 5 of next year. This case shall be reviewed on November 6."

At the same time, the court issued another update to the protection order. Richard could not contact nor come within one hundred feet of Julie and could have no contact with anyone under the age of twenty-one. I thought this was odd since Richard was in jail and couldn't see anyone anyway, but I had nothing to say about it since the courts seemingly knew best.

In the meantime, Sharon received confirmation that DHS had granted an extension to pay for Julie's daycare, and the Kinship program representative, Courtney, continued to keep in touch with Carla and me, asking if there was anything she could do to help. It was a great comfort to know how many people were willing to help since Carla and I really didn't have much, and Carla's pains were increasing daily without resolution.

Richard met with his attorney while in jail. During this time, they decided to delay the dispositional hearing, which would determine whether something had indeed happened to Julie. Carla and I received the answer to that in the mail. The county attorney addressed all the reasons stated for a delay and convinced the courts that a delay was not needed. The trial would proceed, as planned, on September 10th.

The GAL notified me a few days before that I was to testify at the hearing. During the testimony, I was asked to relate what Julie had disclosed to me when she told me the stories about what had happened. I knew that I had an obligation to speak on her behalf. She had been brave enough to disclose what had happened to her, and now it was my turn to be courageous and tell the court what she had said. I knew that Richard would be there and that Richard would now, for the first time, hear what had been told. This didn't make me nervous. What did make me nervous was the thought of breaking down in front of everyone in court. I knew retelling the stories in this stressful situation would cause me to break down, but I had to let them know what was said.

When the day came for court, Carla, Sharon, and I arrived and sat in the courtroom. Richard was brought in wearing his orange jumpsuit and shackles. He looked at Sharon sadly and proceeded to sit next to his attorney. The sight of him in restraints was a stark reminder of the gravity of the situation, and it was hard to reconcile this image with the person I once knew.

The judge entered the room, and everyone stood.

"You may be seated," she said, and everyone did. "This is a dispositional hearing, and it will be sequestered. All witnesses must leave the room until you are called to testify."

I thought I had been confused in the past, but this time, my head was spinning. I decided that after all this was over, I needed to learn more about the law! Why were we being asked to leave? I had no idea that the hearing was going to be sequestered. Sequestered means that the hearing is private, and all witnesses must leave the room until they are called to testify. Honestly, I didn't really even know what that meant. I only knew that I was being asked to wait in the hallway. The original social worker involved with the case was there, and she also stood to leave. At that point, Richard's attorney walked over and whispered to both Sharon and Carla. With confused looks, they both stood and walked out of the courtroom.

I looked up in surprise from my seat by the window. "Why are you two coming out?" I asked. "You weren't called as witnesses."

"Apparently," Carla said, sitting beside me, "Richard's attorney wants us to testify on his behalf. I'm guessing character witnesses."

I could only stare, not knowing what to say. "Um, why would they call you? You are one of the people who Julie disclosed to, and you have never liked him."

"I have no idea," Carla said, looking at Sharon. "She was called as well, so who knows."

Sharon walked over. "I'm not sure what I can say under oath, but I'm guessing that his attorney will come up with questions that will help."

Jill walked out of the courtroom and over to the three of us.

"So, the judge has sequestered the hearing. That means you cannot discuss any testimony between yourselves or with any other witnesses who might come in. You can't talk about this at home or anytime during the trial. Only after the trial is over and done with can you talk about it." Then she turned to me and said, "I'd like to talk with you about the questions I'm going to ask you and how to appropriately respond to any questions that Richard's attorney might ask you in cross-examination. You need to answer his questions but keep your answers short. Just answer limit your answers to address exactly what he asks. Don't volunteer any additional information. Try to keep your voice calm, and don't be argumentative. We don't want you to seem like a hostile witness." This guidance was reassuring, but it also added to the pressure of the situation.

"Okay," I said, my head still spinning. I was uncertain about the questions that would be asked and the testimonies of others. I felt unprepared for the unpredictable nature of what was about to unfold.

"I'll come out and get you when it's time," Jill said, walking back into the courtroom.

I returned to my seat, trying to engage in nervous small talk with Carla and the original caseworker. I observed the constant movement in and out of the courtroom, feeling the tension in the air. When the man who first interviewed Julie hurriedly entered and left the courtroom without making eye contact, the tension seemed to escalate.

A few minutes later, the caseworker was called in, and, as with the interviewer previously seen, she walked out without saying a word and without making eye contact. It was now just Carla, Sharon, and me waiting in the hallway. I paced while Carla and Sharon sat quietly. The creaking of the door to the courtroom entry disturbed the quiet. Jill stuck her head out and motioned for me. "We're ready for you now," she whispered.

I walked into the courtroom following Jill. It was quiet, and all eyes turned toward me as I walked toward the front rail. I stopped at the podium that stood between the two sides of the battle. Richard and his attorney sat on the left. Jill, along with the County Attorney and a stenographer, were on the right. I waited for some cue as to what I should do. I didn't know if I was to sit down or go up to the witness stand. Time seemed to freeze.

The judge, staring at me from her high judge's box, broke the silence. "Mr. Bolton, please come up and stand by the witness box. The clerk will swear you in."

I looked up at the judge. Her smile, though kind, added to the weight of the situation. I had seen her before at another hearing but couldn't remember which one. I walked up to the witness box and stood, facing the clerk.

"Raise your right hand," the clerk said. "Do you swear that the testimony you will give is the truth, the whole truth and nothing but the truth, so help you God? If so, say 'I do'"

"I do," I repeated.

"Please be seated, Mr. Bolton," the judge said, motioning for Jill to proceed.

Jill asked me questions to establish who I was and that I had raised six children. She then asked if Julie had disclosed anything to me while she was staying at my home. I answered affirmatively. She then asked me to please tell the court about the first account. I did. It was difficult to revisit those painful memories, but I knew it was necessary for justice to be served. I made it through. Jill then asked me to tell the court the last story that Julie had told me.

"Sharon was at work," I started out. "She was to be back at the house within the hour. About this time each night, Julie begins to miss her mom and always asks when she'll be home. That night was no exception, but the question was a little differently phrased. Julie asked me, 'When will my mommy and daddy be home?' I told her that her mommy would be home soon. Then Julie asked me, 'What about my daddy?' I had to think. I had to think about what to say. I knew it would just be a matter of time before this question came up, and I was dreading how to answer it. I didn't want to hurt her, and I didn't really know how to explain the why part of it. I figured that it needed to be dealt with sometime, and I thought that at this moment, it might be the time to talk about it. So I told her that her daddy couldn't come to our house and that we would keep her safe."

"And what did she say then, Mr. Bolton?" Jill asked.

I started feeling tightness in my throat and tears welling up in my eyes. It was becoming challenging to speak and difficult to see. The emotional stress was manifesting physically, making it even more difficult to continue. Being a father, I knew what this next statement would mean in the court system and what it would do to the case that

Richard was fighting. Although I felt bad for Richard, as a father, I had to testify what was said. As best I could, I choked through the words that my granddaughter had said to me. "She smiled slightly and looked down at the ground and said, 'Daddy can't hurt me anymore,' and she crawled up on the couch and cuddled with me to finish watching our movie."

Jill looked at her notes and allowed me to regain my composure. "Were you aware that Richard had a previous accusation of sexual assault?"

"Yes, I was aware of that."

"Did it concern you that he was around your family with that accusation?"

"Not too much. He had said that it was a sixteen-year-old girl who looked much older and had been drinking. But then the police told me, after all of this started, that she was actually thirteen and it did concern me, and things started falling into place. I was concerned and I was sad. Concerned for my family and sad that I didn't see the reality sooner. He told me that he didn't know her age and that even the police admitted that she looked older, and that no charges were ever pressed by the parents of the girl."

I felt a little foolish looking back on things at that moment and saying the words out loud. I looked at Richard, who was looking down and shaking his head.

Jill said, "No further questions."

At that point, a wave of relief washed over me at the thought that I was done, but then the judge asked the County Attorney if she had any questions.

"I do, your Honor," and picking up her papers, she walked toward me. *What more could she possibly ask me?* I thought as the nervous feeling in my stomach returned.

CHAPTER 9

Manipulation

❖

She asked a few questions to clarify the previous testimony, and then sat down. Now came the hard part. The judge asked Richard's attorney if he had any questions. I steeled myself against what was to come, when much to my surprise, the attorney stood and said, "I have nothing at this time, your honor," and sat back down. After asking the other two attorneys if they had any further questions and receiving a "no" from both, I was dismissed and asked to wait outside.

As I left the courtroom, I immediately realized why it was that everyone before me had left so quickly having not acknowledged anyone outside. I couldn't talk about what I had said inside, although at this moment in time, I felt the need to talk. The need to get it out and relieve this terrible pain inside. I walked over to Carla with tears welling up in my eyes, sat next to her fighting back what tears were trying to escape.

After a few minutes, all of the attorneys filed out of the courtroom. Jill came over and talked with Carla and I.

"You did very well in there," Jill said to me. "Are you okay?"

"Yeah," I said, "it was just harder than I thought having to tell the stories out loud again. I hope that it helped." My voice shook. I couldn't remember the last time that I had been this upset. This was the turning point for me. Saying out loud what had happened in front of others made it, somehow, more real and more wrong on Richard's part. Saying it out loud made it hurt more, but made the demand for justice a living creature that needed to be satisfied. It broke me down to a small child, but gave me the strength of a superman.

"I think that it did," Jill said. "Please remember that you can't talk about what you said to anyone until this is over."

"I remember, and I won't," I said.

"There is a continuation of this hearing on the 18th at 8 o'clock. Please be here for it. You can all come into the courtroom unless Richard's attorney calls witnesses of his own, at which point you will all need to leave and wait. I'll see you soon."

We all left the courthouse and prepared to come back another day.

Within a week, Sharon received a letter from Richard, addressed to my house. I gave her the letter, reluctantly, and she opened the letter and read it. It was long, and when she was done she sat quietly and sobbed, tears running down her cheeks.

"I'm sorry that this made you sad," I said, trying to comfort my little girl. "What did he say?"

Sharon could speak, but handed the letter to me to read for myself. I sat down next to her and read.

"Dear Sharon,

After two court dates I've seen you at, and after your Dad testified against me, I am not sure where you stand anymore. Your sister's testimony also came out. So between them both, I'm pretty sure where the 'probable cause' came from for my arrest…

Your expression during the last court date was not encouraging. Should I write you off? I don't know anymore. Your Dad lied to me and now this.

Oh, and they removed every penny I have for a 'registration fee'. So now apparently, being arrested and incarcerated against one's will costs over $100 now. So that is why I have been unable to write or call, and since you have not set-up a visit at this point, I'm getting the impression you and the family have written me off. Also, hearing your Dad's testimony of Julie's statements, I am now 100% sure someone has coached Julie. <u>NEVER</u> have I <u>ever</u> hurt our child! In <u>any</u> way. So for your Dad to say what he did, I know someone put that in her little mind that Daddy was hurting her! That makes me sick!

Anyways, I should probably stop talking about it because everything so far points at I have no credibility with you or your family. I could be wrong but body language is not that hard to read.

Even though my chances of winning are extremely slim, I will be going to trial over this most likely. My life is probably over after this point, my beloved. Even if I was to take a plea bargain. You and your family have literally no clue what the possible consequences are or what they put sex offenders and their families through. I've tried to explain before but words honestly do no justice to the horrific treatment they give us. You should have your Dad do a serious investigation with interviews about it.

I also never lied to your Dad about my previous case. I never told him my 'victim' was 16; I said I thought she was sixteen when I was only 18! And, I have yet to see paperwork stating she was under 14! Where is this stuff coming from?! To hear your Dad say that he is now concerned about my past? After hearing all of this from the court date, I'm pretty sure I have to consider your family a loss to me.

The question is are <u>you</u> lost to me? Is it a mistake to call you as a witness in my defense? Do you want me out of yours and our children's lives? What you want is going to decide many things, including whether or not I go to jail for the rest of my life. The law gives you and your family all the backing to either defend or condemn. This is all in your court. Either way, I want to get snipped. No more kids for me. All I get out of being 'Daddy' is pain and broken families. If this situation is ever fixed I will happily continue in that role, but I do not want to bring another child into this world that I cannot be there for.

I am also not going to revoke my power of attorney to you. Please, if you can, get custody of my son. You will give him the most stability and love that he can ever get. He needs that and I doubt I will ever get him at this point. I want all my children to be safe, loved and stable. I'm not sure I can ever provide that anymore. Not from lack of effort, but simply because no matter what I do or don't do I end up in jail too frequently.

This letter is breaking my heart. I love you more than life itself and I will never love another for as long as I live. I keep remembering our last talk together and how you held me through my tears and comforted me. How you told me you would be there for me no matter what as long as you didn't lose the kids.

I have no idea what to think anymore. I feel more alone than ever and I feel betrayed. I feel like just giving up. I am so tired of picking myself up and putting my life back together again. Just before I came in here, I was telling my Dad about how this is my 29th attempt to get my life together, and yet here I am again, in jail. My name is being dragged through the mud. Alone. And in more physical pain than I'm used to dealing with daily. I have at least one seizure every night. Constant migraines. Extreme emotional detachment. Depression on a scale I have never experienced before. And the way things are at this point in time, it's not a matter of 'if ', it's a matter of 'when'.

I can only imagine what you are going through and like I said, I have no idea at all where you stand anymore. Whether it's the same or if it has changed. Having no contact with you is killing me in so many ways. I am so sorry I can't be there for you through all of this, or even be there for the birth of our son. I'm a pretty bad boyfriend, huh?"

Two other letters were enclosed. One was written prior to the hearing, and the other, one day following this last one. It was much shorter and read,

"Sorry that my letters have been so depressing. Right now I am having a very hard time finding anything positive about this situation, and really not knowing what's going on in your head and life right now is causing me all kinds of insecurities, issues and stress.

I MISS YOU! God how I miss you. My life has not been the same since I had to leave your side. I feel incomplete and alone. Do you have any idea how much I love you? With how much of myself that I have trusted you with? More that any single soul in this world, bar none.

You are the light in my dark places!

I do not know who to turn to anymore. My Dad, and you. Those are the only ones I have let into my inner self. I'm scared of what you may be feeling or thinking now though. I won't lie. Every instinct tells me to write you off and run because you are an enemy now, BUT, my instincts were created because of bad people, bad girlfriends, no trust, betrayals and more. I am not wrong to go against my instincts. Praying that you still have me in your heart and your trust.

You are my sunshine, my only sunshine! You make me happy when skies are gray! You'll never know dear, how much I love you! Please don't take my sunshine away!

Please visit. Please write. I need you right now more than I have ever needed anyone before. Love you. Your husband, Richard."

There was another letter included from a date a week earlier. It was pretty much the same and talked about how he was set up, how he wouldn't be there for the birth of his son, how much pain he was in, how much he loved Sharon, and how negative he was feeling about himself. I felt terrible for Sharon. I felt bad because I knew how much these words hurt and tore her up inside. I also felt awful because I could see what I learned that Sharon couldn't see; that Richard had never once, anywhere in these letters, asked for Sharon to let him know how she was doing, how her family was doing, and how the children were doing. There was no concern there for anyone else except Richard. Based on what was in the letters, I felt bad for Richard, and I was sure that Sharon must have felt horrible. I folded the letters up and placed them back in the envelope.

"I'm so sorry, sweetheart," I said. "I'm sure this makes you feel terrible, but we must remember that Julie wouldn't make this stuff up. I'm not sure what to say about what Richard wrote except that we'll all get through it."

"I know, daddy. I'm confused about what happened, my feelings for Richard, and what to think about this and the future. I wish I knew, one hundred percent, what happened or didn't happen," Sharon sobbed.

"Me too, sweetheart. Me too."

Over the next week, I adhered to my usual routine. I escorted my mother to her doctor's appointments, ferried the kids to and from school, drove Carla to work, and dedicated time to my business. Another home visit from the caseworker to check on Julie's well-being came and went, and yet another family meeting was scheduled only to be rescheduled again. Despite the upheaval, we persevered, determined to navigate this storm together.

Even though the hearing had been scheduled, another delay occurred, and the legal system notified our family in the mail that the continuation was moved to October 9th.

Another mail arrived, announcing that Richard's first criminal hearing to determine bail was also set for the 9th. One court hearing in the morning, another in the afternoon. Another day to be spent at the courthouse. I was beginning to feel like I should go to law school just to be compensated for all the time he was consuming. The thought of bail hadn't even crossed my mind. Justice, after all, should be impartial. The law didn't prove him guilty, but our family knew. We had heard. Our hearts had been shattered so many times that I wondered if we would ever feel love, compassion, or trust again. That was the question, at least for me. My god, I was becoming bitter. That wasn't like me. How was I going to cope with this?

Time went by quickly, and before we knew it, the three of us were back in the courtroom, and all the same characters were present. However, this time, it was the defense's turn to present whatever they had. Richard's attorney stood up and argued specific codes with the judge that I certainly had no idea about. The judge smiled, thanked the attorney for his diligence, and then overruled him and asked if he wanted to call any witnesses. To everyone's surprise, he said, "No," and sat beside Richard.

The judge then ruled, saying that she had heard enough evidence to determine that something had indeed happened to Julie at the hand of Richard. She ordered that Richard take the Psychosexual Evaluation once he was out of jail and that he comply with other parts of his ordered therapies.

Earlier that morning, he had appeared in his first criminal hearing and had asked to reduce bail. He was currently in a position where his bail had been set at $100,000. This was an amount that neither he nor his family could handle. His attorney then asked that the bond be set at $10,000. His family could raise the $1,000 needed to bail him out. Carla and I had already spoken with the DA. We agreed that at this point in time, since he had already left the county once, he might try to go again and that we were against the bond reduction. The DA told the judge this information.

After considering everything, the judge reduced the bond to $50,000. This was still too high for his family to handle, and so Richard was to remain in jail. I had no idea at that point in time that Richard would eventually blame me for all of this because of my objection to the bail reduction.

The irony was, had he been granted the bail reduction and bailed out, he would have been obligated to report and start his therapy, or face returning to jail. He vehemently opposed the evaluation, deeming it inhumane and degrading, so my objection had temporarily spared him from that fate. I pondered whether his family could have afforded the bail, and if he would have vanished to evade the evaluation and further legal entanglements. At this juncture, these are questions that will forever remain unanswered.

CHAPTER 10

Normal and Not So Much

❖

Things were becoming routine, in my mind, at least. My daily routines included doing things with Julie, sometimes taking her to the doctor's for check-ups, sometimes picking her up from daycare when Sharon couldn't, and generally juggling the transportation issues.

On October 9th, after the court hearings, I went to the mailbox to get the mail. As I looked through it, I saw a letter from Richard with a return address at the jail, addressed to Sharon again. I wondered if she knew that it was coming. Richard had tried making collect calls to Sharon on several occasions. But she couldn't take the calls because she didn't have the money to pay for them.

When she arrived home that evening, I told her about, and gave her the letter. She opened it and read it. I left the room to give her some privacy, but when I returned, I found my daughter once again in tears. The emotional toll of Richard's actions was evident in every tear that fell from her eyes. I was tired of the hurt that Richard was doling out.

"What's wrong, sweetheart?" I asked her.

"It's just his letter. It makes me very emotional," she said.

"What did he say?" I wondered out loud.

Sharon shared parts of the letter with me.

The letter was much like the others she had received. Richard complained that he still hadn't heard from Sharon. He asked about how their son was doing. He asked Sharon not to discuss his letters with anyone since one of her friends had been noted in the original paperwork, and he didn't know whom she could trust. He then indicated that he knew who that person was.

He said the sentence he would be facing was 38 years to life in prison. He told her he would no longer discuss his case in letter form as he didn't want to be accused of intimidating a witness. He included some samples of his new art style. (I was always very impressed with Richard's artistic talents and wished he could have put them to good use before all of this happened.)

He talked about sadness and anger and how things would not end well. Then he told Sharon how he loved her, missed her and the kids, and wished to be there for them. He didn't sign it as "your husband" this time, but instead just said, "Love you still, love you always…" At the very end of the letter, he wrote, "Did you realize that my son turned five recently? Just another birthday this deadbeat dad missed." This is a reference to his other child with another woman.

Yet another jab at the heart. I sincerely wished that this was just a bad dream.

As a father, I was genuinely conflicted. The weight of the truth, whatever it may be, was heavy on my shoulders. I wanted to know the truth. What really happened? If Richard was innocent and hadn't done anything, he shouldn't be in jail. On the other hand, if Julie's words and stories were valid, then Richard should never be allowed to be near this family again! The allegation, as you may recall, is that Richard has been accused of inappropriate sexual contact with a child. I didn't know what to think. So, I sat down and wrote a letter to Richard. I was always one to put myself in the shoes of other people. I actually think I did this too often and often regretted it. This time, however, I wanted to write to Richard because I needed answers and knew no one had written to him since he had gone to jail. Looking back at that time, I wonder now why I thought that writing to him would get me answers. He would never tell me what happened. Never.

Nonetheless, I sent a letter to Richard:

"Dear Richard:

I wanted to let you know a few things. Sharon has taken the time to read some of your letters to me.

You focus on the fact that someone other than Julie said something to the daycare. If it wasn't accurate, why are you where you are now? Does it really matter who said anything to daycare? Not in my mind. Please read on to see why.

In your letters, you say many things. You talk about how you forgive Sharon. You talk about how you will never see your son. You talk about God. You talk about things that try to turn our focus on feeling sorry for you. At this point, I do feel sorry for you, but not for the reasons you want. Did you know that God talks about repentance? Do you understand what that is? 1. Realizing that you did something wrong. 2. Being sorry for what you did. 3. Confessing your sin. 4. Asking forgiveness. It's not my position to judge, and it's not up to me to forgive, but I can forgive you in my heart. I'm not sure I can ever forget, however.

Julie disclosed numerous things to my family during her first few weeks here. At each disclosure, I cried. At each disclosure, she named you as the person who did these things to her. At each disclosure, my heart broke. If you can explain why it is that Julie would tell 3 different stories to me, 3 other stories to my wife, and at least 3 more to my youngest daughter, not to mention the stories that she told Sharon. A minimum of 11 stories about what happened to her, and stating that you did them. Please tell me why she would say these things over two weeks. I will listen more to what you say.

Julie has no agenda toward you. She never did anything terrible to you. In fact, she loved you. So why would she say these things about you if you did nothing to warrant it? Why would she say, 'Daddy told me I shouldn't tell' and 'Daddy said it was a secret' and 'Daddy said not to tell Mommy because it would make her cry'? Give me a reasonable explanation other than, 'I didn't do anything,' and I will listen more. I have told you this before and will continue with this stand. In the meantime, I must believe Julie, an innocent child who does not have it out for you. In trusting the honesty of what she told me, I am also obligated to speak for her and, in her defense, share what she had to say to me.

The only two people in this world who know the truth are you and Julie. No one else was there. You once asked, 'Who would believe a 3-year-old?' A lot of people do. She convinced me, now it's your turn to tell me why I shouldn't believe her and, instead, listen to you. I still like you, as I've said before, but I still don't like what it appears that you've done to my granddaughter, and I never will. I believe that you need help. Perhaps you don't think this. Maybe you have convinced yourself that nothing happened and that you have become a victim. I don't like the thought of you being forced to change if, in fact, you did nothing wrong. If what Julie is saying is the truth, then this is something you brought on yourself. You make no effort to think of the little girl you hurt. The little girl who would tell me, 'I didn't like it!' when she spoke with me about what you did. Again, why would she say these things, un-prompted, of her own choosing, without being asked? Why would she tell me, 'Daddy can't hurt me anymore,' when she asked if you were coming over, and I told her no, that you weren't allowed to come over anymore?

You continue to claim that you are a victim of circumstance and that others have brought this upon you. The truth is painful. So was what you did to Julie. She will put this away into her subconscious. When she's a teenager, she may need to revisit it in a therapeutic setting. Whether you admit it or not, you will have to live with what you did daily. You might be able to convince others that you did nothing, but those people didn't have to listen to a sweet little girl tell me about what happened. I sincerely hope that through your prayers, you will find the strength to get help. I will pray for you, Richard.

Stephen"

I sent the letter hoping to get some answers and learn the truth. What I saw in the mail a few days later was not what I had hoped for. I had hoped for answers and had received two envelopes. I opened the first, and what I read completely shocked me. The contents of these envelopes, as you will soon discover, were not what I had anticipated. But despite this, my determination to seek the truth remained unwavering.

I expected Richard to be upset, but not to this extent.

I started reading the first letter. It started out, "I am really not sure how to start this letter. I've been meaning to write to you, especially after watching your interview. Still, I keep ending up with angry, disrespectful trash that doesn't get my point across, regardless of my feelings. So, I apologize if I seem curt. I am hurt and angry, but I promise to do my best to not be an asshole."

He continued to defend himself against my testimony in court, where I had spoken out against him based on my granddaughter's account of his actions. He listed the case number of the previous assault and invited me to look up the details. He told me that he had never run from anything. (I wondered if he didn't think going to another county for the weekend based on a bad feeling was considered running.) He then started accusing me of being a liar and dishonest.

He thanked me for treating him as family for a while. He talked about his first plea bargain, with charges being reduced to a felony and 8 to 12 years to life in prison. He continued by saying that everything said about him was a lie and wanted to know what my family, including Sharon, wanted from him.

I was really taken aback by numerous things in the letter. Why did Richard think I was being dishonest? There were a large number of things that made me wonder. There was, however, more to be seen. Within the envelope were two letters; the first one I had just finished was dated November 13, and the second one was dated November 17. I started to read the second letter and steeled myself against the venom that might be unleashed there. The letter started out:

"Dear Stephen:

What do you really say to someone you want to both comfort and to spit on? The look you kept giving me in the court made me feel both anger and empathy to your pain. Then again, what do you really say to someone who is convinced of your guilt and will not be convinced otherwise? And of course is dead set on making you pay for that belief."

I wondered why Richard thought I was so dead on getting him put away. I thought back on the court date and the hearing. I did remember looking at Richard. I was exhausted. I had felt that way for a few days. What did Richard think that I felt with the tired look? Stupid!

I continued to read. The following paragraph blamed me for the fact that Richard would never have custody of his first son. He then talked about how this case was based purely on implications and nothing more. He spoke of his anger toward Julie's GAL and, then again, toward me. Then he started talking about himself and his situation. "Likely I am going away for life regardless of innocence or otherwise…" he said. Then, he began to attack me on a personal level. He said, "…if you think I am being pathetic and dramatic, well, again, I challenge you to take a look for yourself at my past."

I had already decided that I would do that and do my own investigation of what happened with my granddaughter once the trial was over. My granddaughter, just three years old, had bravely recounted the disturbing events she had witnessed involving Richard. Again, I wanted to know in my heart that I was doing the right thing and was not just a puppet whose strings were being pulled. If Richard had indeed done the things that Julie recounted, then he needed to not have contact with my family and deserved an Academy Award for his acting abilities. If he was innocent and someone set him up, then he didn't deserve to be in jail. If only there was a way to know for sure what the truth was. At this point, I still believed my granddaughter. How could I not? How could a three-year-old girl know the details that she told? How could a three-year-old girl tell these stories and then talk about her emotions concerning these stories? There were many questions, but I was determined to find the answers regardless of what it took.

On November 3rd, I received an email saying things were in motion to begin a trial home visit for Julie. Although everyone was excited and this was the day we had all waited for, another day was fast approaching. It actually happened the next day when Sharon went to the hospital and gave birth to her and Richard's son. The birth went well and quickly, with Carla providing unwavering support to Sharon. When Karl was born, Sharon's siblings and I came to see the new addition to the family, offering our love and support. Sharon was sad that Richard couldn't be there.

"As soon as we can," I said, "we must ensure Richard hears about his son. We'll need to check with the lawyers and see what's allowed and what's not."

The next court date was set for November 7th, a crucial day for Sharon to learn about the possibility of a trial homestay. Carla and I found ourselves seated at a table with Jill, Richard's attorney, Larry's attorney, and Sharon's attorney. We couldn't help but feel a bit out of place, being the only ones without a legal background. The magistrate called for a roll call, and Sharon's attorney announced her absence due to the recent birth of her son. The judge's reaction was one of pure joy!

"That's wonderful!" she said. "How are the mother and baby doing?"

"Very well, your honor," Sharon's attorney said.

The Magistrate looked at the paperwork in front of her and asked the caseworker to discuss her recommendation.

"Miss Bolton has been doing everything she's supposed to according to her course of treatment. She's been taking the child, Julie, to therapy. She has been participating in both the parenting classes and her own therapy. I have visited her home, and it's clean, and there are no dangers. With her boyfriend incarcerated, there is no imminent threat to the child. I recommend that she proceed with a trial, at-home visit for thirty days."

The judge asked each of the attorneys if they had any objections or, more accurately, if their clients had any objections. Each was in agreement with the plan.

"Okay," the Magistrate said, smiling, "let's start this today. We'll return in a month and see how things work out."

Carla and I left the courtroom with mixed feelings. Sharon had just given birth, and now they want her to go it alone, taking Julie home and watching a new baby. We knew, of course, that this wouldn't be the case. As we expected, when Sharon left the hospital, she came back to our home to stay and adjust to the new and increased family. Our support was unwavering, providing Sharon with the reassurance she needed.

Julie slept in Kaylie's room the first few nights so that Sharon could deal with the crying baby without waking Julie. On the third night, Julie demanded that she sleep downstairs with Mommy and her new brother, Karl. This adjustment showed Julie's resilience and adaptability, giving us hope for the future.

Things were going well. Sharon had the support of her family and the help she needed to take care of two children. When Julie went to daycare, Sharon would go to her apartment with Karl to clean, move things around, and prepare for the transition. After a couple of weeks, Sharon decided she was ready to try it. She found that Karl wasn't much into sleeping at night and that Julie was an early riser. That, combined with the fact Julie was still getting used to her old but new surroundings, made the nights very long for Sharon. But she was strong and did what she could.

When the social worker and Jill came for a home visit a few days later, they were both very impressed with how Sharon managed to keep the house in order and care for her children. They were sure they had made the right decision to allow Sharon to try this. They had no reservations about recommending she receive permanent custody again at the next hearing. The only concerns they had were about how Sharon felt about Richard. Even though she openly said she didn't want to have him around Julie anymore, there was still the consensus that she had feelings for him and would have trouble with that commitment if he were released. Who could blame her, though? They had been close, made plans, talked about their future together, and even considered marriage at one point. He had been good to her. According to Sharon, he was better than any of her previous boyfriends. It was difficult for her to come to grips with the fact that he might have hurt her little girl in any way. To make things worse, Julie had started talking about Richard. She wondered where he was and would talk about the fun things they did together. She would say that she missed him and wanted a Daddy again. Then Sharon would think back about how her sister, when she was younger and following her assault, would talk about missing the family member who assaulted her. She would cry at night because she missed him.

"I think it's just part of the process," I told her. "I'm not sure why. I'm not a psychiatrist. As adults, we would expect to loathe someone who hurt us so much that we needed to tell them and report what happened. It must be somewhat different with children. It would be interesting to find out why someday."

Sharon agreed thoughtfully, but I imagined how hard it still must be for her to be torn up inside and not know how to come to grips with what could be a horrible truth. We felt a deep sense of empathy for Sharon's struggle.

Richard wrote another of his regular letters to Sharon on November 10th. As always it came to my house and, as always, I gave it to Sharon and waited until the tears started to flow, then comforted her in her sorrow.

She handed me the letter, and I read the all too familiar words that were neatly written on the pages:

"Dear Sharon:

Hmmm.. Hello and congratulations I have no idea when our baby was born or his name or any detail about him. Or whether my name is on the birth certificate. I can't tell you how sorry I am to not be there for that. It's been keeping me awake at night and eating lean for months now.

What does our baby (boy right?) look like? Can I get a picture? When was he born? How big was he? What is his name? How long was labor? Who was there? Are you okay? Any complications?

I could easily ask 10,000 more questions, but I'm not sure if I would ever get an answer. IF you had picked up the phone in the past 6 weeks, I would never know since the call is never confirmed. You said you would be there. Then again, so did your parents and they are why I am in jail.

So, if you are in that bandwagon (I don't know cause your last police interview tape is missing so far) I apologize for 'forgiving' you and I say this because it would be pretty damn arrogant of me to shove at you. And since I have had zero feedback, I am just going off what I can read. Or in several cases, whatever you tell or don't tell my father.

I won't lie. I am miserable. I turned 31 without a single 'Happy Birthday' from anyone, not even my own father. My mom and dad have both promised money for hygiene and stamps. I have been here 70 days now. No letters. No calls. Very few visits from my Dad only. And more broken promises than I can count from everyone I trusted. I don't know why I try and trust anyone anymore. Or try to prove anything. People are paranoid, evil, and selfish and will do, say, and believe whatever they want regardless of consequences or truth.

Ok, ok. I promised myself not to make this into another shitty despondent letter. I apologize.

Well, regardless of what you believe, I still love you. I love Julie. I love our baby boy. I miss you and the kids. Honestly, I just miss being trusted by those I love. But worst of all, I miss being happy. Real and true happy.

I'm asking for some answers now. My Dad told me something that not even he can believe about them taking Julie away from you for contacting me. (Not meant to be rude.) I have the right to know a few things. I need closure. Either closure on 'us and family' or closure on how I feel and hope for a future.

Nit and grit is this: my first plea bargain thrown at me was 8-12 years DOC (prison). I am facing 48 to LIFE. Thanks to your parents. Thanks to the concerted effort of everyone against me. (Yes, that is Meredith who STARTED all of this at daycare).

Do I have hope of ever seeing my son? You? Julie? Or do I need to cut ties and leave you all to 'heal' over whatever you think I did? Answer to the last, only you can give me. And it is what I need to know to myself together. Cause am I alone? You and EVERYONE else told me I wasn't…cause 70 days (10 weeks) later, so far, I am. I can't even get anyone to acknowledge my existence. I feel hated.

Ugh,…sorry again. I am very conflicted and I don't handle that well. I am sorry. Who does our boy look like the most? Color of hair/eyes? PLEASE tell me. And please tell me what you want.

You matter to me. As do your opinions. I am sorry if there was any doubt of that. And I am sorry from the bottom of my soul that you have to go through this. I love you. Please write me or have someone else tell me about our baby and WTF is going on.

Always yours, (If you'll have me) Richard

P.S. Today I confirmed our kid's birth and nothing else. And EXACTLY to the day 13 years ago I made the mistake that put my life under the law and my name in the trash. Crazy coincidence. I'm crying. I love you. I am so sorry."

Sigh.

CHAPTER 11

Court Hearings Again

❖

I thought about the letter I had just read and about the letters Richard had sent before. There was never an expression of concern for Sharon. He never once asked how Sharon was doing or how Julie was doing. He continued to say things to make Sharon feel sorry for him and to blame others for what was going on with him. Mostly, Richard never offered an apology! He shifted the blame, indicating it was Carla's and my fault. I again shook his head.

How could this be our fault? I wondered, and then I realized Richard was saying that his being in jail was the fault of the entire family. If we hadn't said what happened, he would never have been exposed, caught, or put in jail! This realization made me angry, and I felt foolish for feeling sorry for this man.

Carla, Sharon, and I went to court on December 18th. This was to be Richard's preliminary hearing. From what Richard had said in his letter to Sharon, we were expecting his attorney to announce that they had accepted the deal. We arrived at 1:45 in the afternoon and checked the docket. Richard was listed with one other person who was scheduled for sentencing. We walked into the courtroom and sat down.

The other person being sentenced was first. I thought it shouldn't take too long, but instead, a witness was called to testify, followed by a 'phone tap' recording. This continued for an hour and a half. To my dismay, I had to leave to pick up the kids from school. They had been waiting for over an hour but had been told that morning I would be late. But not this late.

"I have to go get the kids soon," I whispered to Carla. "They can't stay at school past four."

"Then you'd better leave now," she replied.

I got up and quietly left the courtroom.

When I arrived at the first school, I texted Carla, "Have they finished up yet?"

Carla replied, "The two attorneys are starting their closing statements. I don't think this should take very long."

At the second school, I sent another text. "How are things going?"

Carla replied, "They are still finishing up their closing arguments."

I drove as quickly as I could to get the kids home, then hurried to the parking garage near the courthouse. I looked at my phone and noticed that I had a text from Carla that read, "We're going down to the second floor."

"Why?" I replied but received no response. Then I sent, "I've just parked. I'll be there shortly."

The reply confused me, as the delay in texts sometimes does. "We're heading to the front door. Just pick me up there."

I immediately ran to the front doors and found Carla waiting. "What happened?" I asked.

We started walking toward the parking garage, as Carla explained. "After the 'drug person' was sentenced, they called another case, but it wasn't for Richard. So, I spoke with the DA, and she told me to go to the DA's office on the second floor to find out what was happening. When I got there, I spoke with the DA advocate. She checked and said it looked like the court hearing had been 'continued,' but she couldn't tell why or when the next court date was."

That's strange," I said.

When I got home, I emailed Jill, Julie's GAL. She was always there for us regarding legal matters, and I knew it would be her if anyone could help. The email read,

"Dear Jill. So, Carla, Sharon, and I went to court today. We had the opportunity to see a woman who was convicted of dealing drugs in our city and sentenced to 20 years in prison. Great for the kids in our town!

Richard's case was not called after that, even though he was the only other case on that docket. I had to leave toward the end of the drug lady's sentencing to pick up our kids from school, so Carla went down to speak with the DA advocate to find out why Richard's case wasn't called. They hmmm'd and hawed and couldn't figure it out, only saying that it looked like it had been continued, but for what reason they weren't sure. Do you have any insight into this and for what date it has been rescheduled?

Thanks as always for everything you do for us! I can't tell you enough how much we appreciate you.

We are hopeful that with your help, we can navigate this situation successfully. Hope to hear from you soon.

Jill is an amazing attorney who is accommodating and helpful. The next morning, I received a response in my mailbox. It read,

"Hi Stephen,

How odd! I ended up getting caught in court and didn't make it down. I spoke with the DA earlier in the week who indicated that Richard was trying to get the DA to offer a determinate sentence (basically putting a cap on the maximum time in jail) but that he thought there would be an agreement soon.

Perhaps they've reached an agreement and didn't feel a preliminary hearing was necessary. A prelim is a hearing about the trial and often just encompasses details of how the trial plays out procedurally, and allows the parties to get different deadlines for motions to exclude or introduce certain evidence at the actual hearing. If the case isn't going to trial, there's no need for a prelim. I'll follow up with the DA today and let you know what's going on. I don't see a new date in the computer yet.

Thanks,

Jill"

At this point, I could do nothing but wait for her update.

A few days later, she replied with a new court date. The next hearing was set for January 8th. This meant that the family would be attending two more court dates in a row, January 7th for the D&N hearing and then again on January 8th for the criminal case. Both hearings were set for 2 p.m. each day. My biggest concern about this was that Carla would need to take two afternoons off of work, and I would have to tell the kids I couldn't pick them up on time each day. Things would work out, however, and all would be figured out.

A week later, I was out working on a Saturday. When I arrived home, Carla approached me.

"Someone came to the door," she said concernedly. "It was an older gentleman that I didn't know, so I didn't answer."

"I wonder who it was," I asked.

"I don't know," Carla said, "but he had a stack of papers that he was going through in the car. I think he might have been a process server."

"Well, I guess if he really needs to talk with us, he'll be back," I said, shrugging it off.

The next day, I heard a car pull up in front of the house. I looked out the window and saw a nice car parked on the street with an older man sitting behind the wheel, going through papers. I sighed and went to Carla.

"It seems your enigmatic visitor has returned," I remarked, adding to the air of mystery.

Carla looked out of the window and nodded. "That's the car that was here yesterday," she said.

"I may as well go out and see what he wants," I said, heading toward the front door.

I walked outside and down the street and noticed that the man was still going through papers. I was approaching the car when the man got out. He hadn't seen me walking toward him, and my sudden appearance startled the man.

"Oh, goodness!" the man said.

"Can I help you?" I asked.

"Um, yeah. Are you Stephen?" the man asked.

I sighed, "Yes, I am."

The man held out a paper. "I imagine that you're expecting this," he said. "It's a subpoena."

I looked it over, but the smaller writing was difficult to make out without my reading glasses.

The older man continued, "And the wife? Is she at home?"

"She's upstairs," I said, still trying to determine what I was being subpoenaed for.

"Would it be okay if I just gave hers to you?" the man asked.

"Sure. Why not?" I replied and took the other paper.

"Thank you," the man said. "Have a good day."

The man got back in his car and drove away. I went into the house. I know it's probably out of habit or being polite, but why would someone give me court papers and tell me to have a good day? Unless the judge will pay me millions of dollars, I can't imagine that being forced to come to court fits in with having a good day.

"We've been subpoenaed," I told Carla, handing her the papers.

"What is this for?" she asked.

"I think it's for the Disposition hearing," I said.

Later that day, Sharon came over, and I told her about the subpoena. Sharon looked at it.

"This is for the D&N hearing," she said.

"Why would we need to testify at that?" I wondered aloud. "I thought they just wanted to discuss the protection order."

"That is strange," Sharon said.

Little did we know, a twist was about to unfold.

A little before Christmas, I received a phone message from the County Attorney's office requesting a time to speak with Carla and me about the upcoming hearing and why we had been required to appear in court. I looked at my calendar, found a good time the next day, and called back to schedule the meeting. When I was ready and with Carla, I called back. I was driving Carla to work and anticipated giving the phone to her when needed, but the need never arose. The County Attorney asked about the letters that Richard had sent to Sharon and to me. After the conversation ended, Carla said she would like to speak with the attorney face to face to see what this was all about.

I promptly arranged a meeting for the 23rd, two days before Christmas, sparking anticipation for what was to come.

When Carla and I met with her, the County Attorney answered all of Carla's questions and then turned to me.

"I'm only going to call you to testify at this hearing," she said, "since Richard has only written to you and Sharon. I want you to testify about the contents of the letters and Sharon's reactions to the letters. I propose you act as an intermediary in the letter between Richard and Sharon. Richard can write to you, and you can pass along messages to Sharon. Sharon can give you things to tell Richard. I would also like you to be able to update Richard on his son. It's only fair that he should know how his son is doing. Would you be willing to do that?"

"Of course," I said without hesitation. "As a father, I can imagine the pain he's in not being able to be there for his son, but at the same time, as a father, I want to protect my daughter from any further emotional upset."

"I've presented the idea to Richard's attorney. He's not happy about the idea yet, but we'll see what happens," the attorney said.

"Let me know," I said. "I'll help in any way I can."

As we left in the bitter cold, I was not happy that I would once again have to sit in the witness box and testify. Still, I hoped that it would help my daughter heal and Richard stop writing things to make her cry.

Christmas came and went. We had no money this year, and Christmas was sparse at best, but the family was together, and that's all that mattered to me. Everyone was healthy, and their hearts were filled with joy. Well, not everyone was healthy. Bertran was having some problems. Sharon had taken him to the emergency room because of severe pain. Over the next few weeks, he went back four more times. I had taken him to get his prescriptions and paid for them. I also bought him lunch because I was concerned about his eating habits. While eating and waiting for the prescriptions, I told him the stories that Julie had told me. Bertran looked shocked and agreed that something must have happened to her. A week or so later, I heard Bertran say the same thing to Sharon, with a slight twist.

"After what your dad told me about what Julie said, I'm sure that something happened to her," Bertran said. "I can't believe it was my son, though, so it must have been someone at the daycare that did it."

Inside, I just shook my head. I would ask around once the trial was over and get to the truth. Still, if the truth pointed to Richard as a perpetrator, as I suspected it would, Bertran would never accept it. I would find out who told whom first and how this all began. For now, I would bide my time and wait patiently.

On New Year's Day, I received a phone call from Bertran. "You mentioned the other day that you could, perhaps, take me to get a money order for my rent. Is that something we could do today?"

"Of course," I said reassuringly. "Give me a few minutes, and I'll head over there to get you."

I dropped what I was doing and told Carla I was going over to help Bertran. Carla wasn't feeling well and just nodded based on what she heard.

"I love you," I said.

"I love you too," Carla replied.

I drove over to Bertran's house, and when I went to the door, Bertran was getting his things together.

"How are you feeling?" I asked, my concern for his health evident in my voice. "You're looking like you're feeling better."

"Not really," Bertran replied, his voice betraying his discomfort. "I'm still not feeling very well. I don't know what I'm going to do."

"I'm so sorry you're not doing well," I said, offering my support. "Let's go get you that money order and get you back here so that you can get some rest."

We headed out to the car. I kept feeling that I should take Bertran's arm and help him walk, just as I did with my mother, but I knew Bertran was doing fine and didn't need the help.

I drove down to the local grocery store, where I knew the rates for money orders were the lowest. We exited the car, and I noticed Bertran looking around, confused. "What are you looking for?" I asked.

"My bank," Bertran replied.

"Did you want to get the money order at your bank?"

"Well, I guess I can," Bertran said.

I suddenly realized and asked, "Did you get the money from the bank yet?"

"No. I'm sorry I didn't let you know. My bank is inside the other grocery store on the north side of town."

"No problem," I said, admiring his determination. "We'll drive up there and get you some cash and the money order."

As I drove, I asked some questions. "Have you had the chance to talk with Richard recently? I know things have been difficult between you two."

"No," Bertran said. "I never have the chance to get down there."

"Let me know if you need a ride," I said. "I can take you. Has Sharon filled you in on the deal they're offering him?"

"Yeah, she told me. It's a joke. Two to eight years for something Richard didn't do. After you and I spoke, I realized something definitely happened to Julie. Still, I now know that blaming Sharon's friend was a mistake. She actually called the police to report that Julie was being abused by the daycare. Most people don't know that the daycare is still under investigation!" Bertran seemed very sincere in his statement.

"Really?" I said. "How do you know this?"

"It's in the paperwork," Bertran said matter-of-factly.

"You have the paperwork from the police?" I asked.

"Oh yeah," Bertran said. "I was going to show that part to Sharon when she was over the other day, but I couldn't find it. I'm going to keep looking."

I made a mental note to speak with Sharon about what Bertran told me. "So you mentioned the two to eight years," I said. "That was the old deal. Now it's twelve to twenty-four years. I told Sharon that he should have taken the first deal and that he should have turned himself in instead of leaving the county that weekend."

"Oh, he never left the county," Bertran said. "I've always told him to face up to his responsibilities and never run away from them."

"Sharon told me that he left the county because of a bad feeling."

"He wanted to," Bertran reflected, "but I convinced him not to. He was gone that weekend but went to his friend's house just south of here. He was still in the county. In fact, the day that he was arrested, we were on our way to the police station so that he could turn himself in. He had called earlier in July and told the police that he was coming down to turn himself in, but they lied to him and said he didn't have to because there was no warrant out for his arrest. He only found out that there was a warrant because he went online and checked. The officer that arrested him was very nice. He told me that he understood this was my son and he would do this quietly and gently. Then Sharon came to help me. I don't know what I would have done without her help."

I told Bertran I had written to Richard and updated him on Bertran's health. Bertran expressed his appreciation.

"I'm going to send Richard a letter tomorrow. Is there anything that you'd like me to tell him for you?"

"Just keep him updated about my health," he said.

"Does Richard have your phone number, Bertran?"

There was a noticeable silence following that question, and then Bertran answered. "No."

"Would you like me to send that to him?"

Again, there was a noticeable silence. "That would be very kind of you," Bertran said.

We pulled into the grocery store's parking lot and headed inside. As we approached the doors, I realized what day it was.

"Bertran, I don't think your bank will be open today," I said.

"Why not?"

"It's New Year's Day," I replied.

Bertran thought about it. "It might be open," he said. "It's inside the grocery store, which is open."

So we continued inside and found that the bank was closed. Bertran tried using the ATM but couldn't remember the PIN. As we headed toward the door, Bertran asked if he could do some shopping. So we took the time to shop for groceries and then drove over to the dollar store. By the time we were done, Bertran was happy and loaded with food and essentials.

I dropped Bertran off at his house and carried in his groceries.

I promised, "I'll swing by again tomorrow and take you to the bank so you can pay your rent."

"I appreciate it," Bertran said. I'll see you tomorrow."

I drove home and spoke with Sharon, who had brought the kids to the house for a visit. She shook her head when I relayed the stories that Bertran had conveyed.

"I know that Richard was out of the county, and I also know that he wasn't on his way to the police station when he was arrested. He was on the other side of town headed away from the police station."

I sighed. "There seems to be a lot of lies or misinformation in this case, but I'm glad you could verify that what you originally told me was the truth. What about the daycare?"

"I haven't heard anything," she said, "but I'm sure I would know if they were under investigation."

"When this case is over, that is the first place I'm going to interview. I still think that the daycare is where it all started!"

True to my word, I sent a letter to Richard the next day. In it, I told Richard about his father and the neuropathy issues he was having. I talked about Richard's son and even printed a photo of him. Nowhere in the letter did I say anything about myself. I was done dealing with the ire in the replies I received from Richard, who had convinced himself that I was only in this to see him "pay for what he had done…" I knew otherwise but would not say another word to Richard about myself. I am eager to see the court case end to begin talking with people and find out what happened. I knew the following Monday Sharon was in for a rude awakening. I had been told that Julie's therapist was ready to tell Sharon something had happened. I wasn't told the extent of what the therapist would say, and I was eager to hear what Sharon would say in three days. It was so close but seemed so far away. I knew, however, that patience was the key. Waiting for the truth was sometimes challenging but totally worth it in the end, no matter what you considered the truth to be at the time.

Two days later, I couldn't get a hold of my mother, who had been struggling with her health. I went over to her apartment, let myself in, and found that she had passed away. Now, in addition to dealing with everything else, I was faced with moving things out of Mom's apartment, taking care of the funeral arrangements, and finding time to grieve. I was getting good at grieving.

CHAPTER 12

Nearing the End

❖

On January 7th, Carla, Sharon, and I returned to the courtroom. It was time for the civil hearing and determination as to whether the order of protection should be extended to include Sharon. This would mean that Richard wouldn't be allowed to write to Sharon and would need to obtain information about his son through a third party. I was more than likely going to be that person.

The caseworker testified about how Sharon's letters from Richard had affected her. I provided a similar testimony. Richard was not present in the courtroom but was on the telephone from the jail. When it came time for Richard to speak, his attorney went to the podium to interview him, there was tension in the air.

"Mr. Pantane," the attorney spoke, "it has been suggested that you receive information about your son, Karl, through Mr. Bolton. How would you feel about that?"

There was a silence over the speakerphone for a moment, and then Richard spoke up. His words carried a heavy emotional weight. "I would not like that. In fact, I find it completely unacceptable."

"And why is that, Mr. Pantane?

"I don't trust Stephen. I don't think he would send me accurate information about my son. I love Sharon, and I don't think there's any reason I can't contact her. However, if I'm not allowed to do that, I want my mother to be the go-between."

I thought that there was something really wrong with what Richard was asking. During his entire time in jail thus far, Richard had received no communication from his mother, no letters, calls, or personal visits. I was sure that part of the reason had to do with the fact that Richard's mom lived almost 200 miles away.

Richard and his attorney continued their conversation for several minutes, attempting to establish what Richard wanted and what he thought was right. Once that was all defined, it was time for cross-examination.

The County Attorney asked questions about how Richard was attempting to manipulate Sharon and Stephen in his letters. The GAL told Richard that his communication with Sharon was not good for Julie. Then, it was Sharon's attorney's turn.

Sharon's attorney stood at the podium and looked over his notes. "Mr. Pantane," he started. "I'm Sharon's attorney. You claim that you love Sharon and are only interested in her best interests, correct?"

"Yes," Richard's voice said quietly over the phone speaker.

"What if I were to tell you that Sharon doesn't want to communicate with you anymore?"

"I haven't heard if that's the case," Richard said.

"Mr. Pantane," the attorney said more forcefully, "I'm telling you now that Miss Bolton does not want to communicate with you at all."

At that point, Sharon stood up and left the room quickly. Carla and I looked at each other.

"You should go out and ensure she's okay," I said. "I must stay in the courtroom since I'm a witness."

Carla stood up and left the courtroom to follow her daughter.

Richard's attorney stood. "Your honor, I want the record to reflect that immediately after that last statement, Miss Bolton and her mother left the courtroom." He sat down, and the caseworker immediately stood up and left the courtroom. Richard's attorney stood once again and addressed the court. "Your Honor, I want the record to reflect that the caseworker has left the courtroom now."

The judge looked at the attorney. "I can note that the caseworker has left the courtroom as she is a witness in this case; however, to my knowledge, Mrs. Bolton and her daughter are not witnesses and are only sitting in the gallery. As you know, people sitting there are welcome to come and go as they please."

The judge looked at the County Attorney, who shook her head, indicating that neither Sharon nor her mother were to testify.

The judge said, "Let the record indicate that the caseworker left the room immediately following the statement. You may continue, Mr. Howard."

Sharon's attorney asked the judge if he could speak with his client for three minutes. The judge granted the request, and Mr. Howard left the court. In some comedic part of my mind, I half expected that Richard's attorney would stand and ask that the record indicate that Sharon's attorney had left the court, but he didn't.

Mr. Howard found Sharon and Carla just outside of the courtroom, talking. (Apparently, the caseworker had a different stop to make.) Sharon was fighting back tears.

"So, Sharon, do you want to continue communicating with Richard?" Mr. Howard asked.

"I just don't think it will hurt anything if I continue to write to him and have him write to me," Sharon said.

"I strongly recommend that you don't say that in the courtroom," Mr. Howard said. "It will make you look like a bad mother in front of the judge and caseworker. You need to give the impression, at least, that you don't want to have anything to do with him."

"But that's not what I want," she replied.

Mr. Howard pursed his lips. "I need to do what's best for you and your daughter," he said, and walked back into the courtroom.

After Mr. Howard re-entered the room, he walked up to the podium. Sharon, Carla, and the caseworker also returned and took their seats. Mr. Howard indicated that he was ready to resume, and the judge nodded her approval.

"Mr. Pantane, Miss Bolton no longer wants to communicate with you. Will you honor that?"

I turned to look at Sharon. She had her head down and was resting against the bench. I walked back and whispered, "Are you okay?"

"I don't know," was her response. "That's not what I told my attorney. He's not saying what I wanted. He's saying what he thinks would be best for the court to hear."

I went back to my seat. Carla had left to pick up the kids from school. I realized that Sharon had been playing both ends against the middle. She would say what needed to be said and what needed to be heard. I suggested that Sharon take the stand and say what she felt.

"If I do that," Sharon said, "they'll think I'm a bad mother and take the kids away from me again."

I realized that Sharon couldn't take the stand because what she had told Richard, her parents, and the attorneys and caseworkers were stories that were all different in content and meaning. Taking the stand would mean the loss of something or many things. So, for now, it meant staying quiet and fixing things later.

When the attorneys were asked to give their closing statements, they went in the order that they had done previously for questioning. I listened to each one restate what they had already brought up, but then Julie's GAL stood up and spoke. My ears perked up when he heard her say something about being broken.

"There is so much that is broken in this case," she said to the judge. "Richard is broken. Sharon is broken. Julie is broken. Carla and Stephen are broken. The family has been broken by the act of one person, and the family needs to be fixed. However, it cannot be fixed if contact continues with Mr. Pantane by Miss Bolton. If contact can be broken, the healing can begin for Miss Bolton and, most importantly, for the child, Julie."

Once all the attorneys had given their closing statements, the judge smiled and looked at the court. She sighed and said, "I need time to think about this. We will reconvene again on January 13th at 1:00 p.m. when I present my decision."

"All rise," the clerk said, standing in her little box beside the judge. The judge smiled and stood again, then turned and left the courtroom. Richard had already hung up the phone. I went with Sharon, hugged her goodbye, and stood in the cold, waiting for Carla to arrive with the kids.

I explained what was going to happen to Carla on the way home.

Carla sighed, "You mean I have to take more time off work?"

"I can go," I said, "and tell you what is said. It should be the final hearing."

It would be the final hearing in the civil case, but tomorrow, Carla, Sharon, and I would be back in the courtroom again to hear the criminal case and a preliminary hearing for Richard. It was going to be a long week.

The next day, everyone was back, including Richard. He sat next to his attorney but stood when the judge entered. Bertran and Sharon sat in the front row while Carla and I sat just behind them. The judge sat down and asked Richard's attorney which of the two cases of the day he wanted to work on first. The attorney indicated that Richard should go first.

They both stood and approached the podium. The attorney indicated to the judge that they had been negotiating a plea with the D.A., stating they had almost reached an agreement. He asked the judge if they could schedule the hearing for the following week.

"Let's convene on January 15th at 11:00 in the morning. Will that work for everyone?" the judge asked.

I thought the judge was asking only the attorneys. Both attorneys agreed they could meet then, and the case was recessed until then.

The District Attorney for this hearing walked to the back of the courtroom and asked Carla if she was there for Richard's case. Carla nodded. Neither she nor I had seen this attorney before. He said that he wanted to speak with us. I was trying to return the hearing aid the court provided me to help with my poor hearing. By the time I made it out, the District Attorney had already started speaking with Carla. Bertran had followed me and ambled over to a bench to sit. I couldn't help but notice, with some amusement, that Bertran was leaning toward the conversation.

"…so I want the advocate to contact you," the District Attorney, Sam, was already talking with Carla. "We want you to know what their counteroffer is prior to court, to make sure that you approve."

I stuck out my hand. "I'm Stephen Bolton," I told the DA, and we shook hands. "Thank you for keeping us updated on what's going on."

"My pleasure," Sam said. "I want to meet with all of you before the next court date. I'm hoping that will be a possibility. The advocate will be in touch very soon."

I walked over to Bertran and helped him to stand, and we all left the courthouse together.

The next day, I checked my email and received one from the DA's Advocate, Sasha. In this email, which was also sent to Sharon, Carla, Jill, and the caseworker, Sasha asked if we could all meet in the DA's office on Monday, Tuesday, or Wednesday the following week. She said that the DA wanted to make sure everyone knew what the counteroffer was and what the consequences would be if the case went to trial.

Once we had all agreed on Tuesday morning, we arrived and were escorted back to a conference room in the DA's office complex.

Our collective decision to meet on Tuesday morning made us all feel part of the process.

Once everyone was seated, no one spoke. The silence in the room was ominous, indicating that something serious was about to be discussed. Sam spoke up first, breaking the tension.

"After the last offer, they came back with a counteroffer. Ten years. We countered with ten to fourteen years. I wish that I could ask for something different. I mean, I'd like to see Richard get out and on probation and get some treatment options, but because he's a repeat offender, my hands are tied as far as what I can ask for."

He went on to talk about the fact that he would only serve half of his sentence in prison and possibly not even that much. There were formulas that the Department of Corrections talked about having. Still, they seemed secret, and Sam couldn't figure them out.

Sharon said, "Richard is concerned about never coming out of prison alive. He said sex offenders, especially child molesters, are targeted and killed."

Sam almost laughed. "I've been doing this a long time. How many times do you read in the paper about a sex offender who was killed in jail?" When there was no reply, he continued. "That's a very common thought, but the reality is I see sex offenders come out of prison all of the time, and I've never heard of anyone getting killed."

Carla asked about what might happen if Richard decided not to take the deal being offered.

"Right now, it looks like he's going to accept the deal," Sam said. "If he decided to take it to a jury trial and he didn't win, then he'd be looking at thirty-five years to life in prison. I'm sure he doesn't want to risk it. If he decides not to take the plea bargain, however, it would mean that Julie would have to take the stand and testify."

"But she's only three years old," Carla said.

"Still, the law states that the accused has the right to face his accuser."

"Will he be in the room?" Carla asked.

"Unfortunately, he'll be there sitting fifteen feet away from her. First, the judge will need to conduct a competency test to see if she is, in fact, competent to testify. If Julie is deemed competent, she'll be questioned by the attorney for the people, me, and then cross-examined. Only after she testifies will the court watch her forensic interview, and you will all be called to testify about what she told you. It's never pleasant to have to interview a child that young, and I've seen it go both ways. Some kids are great with it, while others just shut down. She might surprise you."

Carla grabbed a Kleenex and wiped away the tears beginning to run down her face. Julie had been through so much already, and Carla, nobody in that room really wanted to see her go through anymore. Would this traumatize her even more? We could only wait and see what would happen. The DA seemed convinced that Richard would take the deal. None of us knew what I would be told that evening. I would hear something that would turn our worlds inside out.

In the afternoon, Sharon and I went to the civil hearing, where the judge would read what she had decided about the extended protection order. Everyone stood as the Magistrate entered the room. When we were all seated, she read, out loud, her notes from the previous week's hearing. The Magistrate decided that Richard only wanted to hear about his son and how he was doing. To accomplish this, she said that Sharon could write to Richard but that Richard could neither respond nor contact her in return. He was also to not ask anyone to deliver any messages to her. It was a wise solution; all attorneys agreed to the new order.

That evening, I had promised Bertran that I would drive him down to the jail so he could have a half-hour visit with his son. Bertran was hurting and not doing well but seemed excited at the prospect of the visitation.

My mother had passed away the week before and had left a lovely cane, one of the self-standing types, and had told me to give her belongings away to anyone who really needed them. After dropping Bertran off at the jail, I went home and got the cane to give him, then returned to the prison to pick him up.

I didn't have to wait long for Bertran to come out. He got in the car, and I gave him the cane.

"Oh, thank you so much for this!" Bertran said. "It will really help."

"Mom said to give her things to people in need, and I thought you needed this more than anyone I knew."

We started to drive off, and I asked, "How is Richard doing?"

"Well, as you might imagine, he's angry and alone. He feels as if everyone has deserted him," Bertran said.

"I can't imagine being in that situation," I said. "I've never been in jail, but I can't imagine it's pleasant."

"They just let him into the general population," Bertran said sadly. "He's already receiving death threats."

"What?" I was shocked. I never thought these things really happened, especially in County Jail and after what the D.A. had told them all today. "I'm so sorry to hear that. Did he say anything about taking the deal?"

"He's not going to take the deal," Bertran said.

I could physically feel my entire body go numb. The world felt like it slowed, and nothing made sense anymore.

"I don't understand," I said. "I thought Richard wanted to take it."

"I told him not to. My father was a police officer who always told me that if I was ever in trouble and had to go to jail, I should never take a deal. He told me that if they offer a deal, they have nothing on you. This entire case is based on hearsay, with no physical evidence. He can beat it."

I realized that I was in a minor state of shock. "You told him not to take the deal? Do you know what that means for the rest of us? It means that everyone in my family will be subpoenaed to testify. Even Julie must take the stand in front of everyone, including Richard, and tell what he did."

Bertran turned to look at me. "Why would they put a three-year-old girl on the stand?"

"According to the law, the accused has the right to face his accuser," I said.

"But she didn't accuse him!" Bertran said, "It was Sharon's friend."

"That's not how the authorities are viewing it, Bertran. They are saying that Julie was the one who accused him. They are saying that she said something to the people at daycare. Because she's been telling us her stories and disclosing information, she is the accuser, so she has to testify."

Bertran sat quietly, shaking his head. "Oh my God. How could they do this to a little three-year-old girl?"

I thought to myself, *How could your son, a man who was supposed to protect her, do what he did to a three-year-old girl?*

"Bertran, you need to tell Richard to take the deal," I said quietly.

"I don't think he will, but I'll try."

All I could think was, *what will the uncertain future hold?*

CHAPTER 13

How Do You Plead?

❖

A few weeks passed, and the family was worried about what would happen. The District Attorney and the Public Defender went back and forth during the bargaining. The latest was now ten to fourteen years, with a change in charges, lowering them somewhat.

Finally, the day came for the preliminary hearing to occur again. Carla, Sharon, and I arrived early, but the doors to the courtroom were locked.

I joked.

Carla sat.

Sharon paced.

Eventually, someone unlocked the courtroom door. I insisted we go in and sit down, but Carla wanted to wait. Just as she said we should wait, we heard the DA, his assistants, and the detective from the case coming down the hallway. The detective walked up and gave them all hugs.

"It's good to see you guys! How are you holding up, and how is Julie doing?"

"She's back in the custody of Sharon," Carla said, "and we're all holding up as best we can. Just ready for this all to be over."

Cheryl smiled. "I'm glad that some things are returning to normal and that Julie is back home. That's wonderful."

I was tired, as had been the case a lot over the past several months, and ready to get inside and get things going. "Shall we all go in?" I asked.

The DA looked at me. "I'm going to have to ask that all of you wait out here," he said. "Since you all are potential witnesses, and there will more than likely be a gag order on this case from the judge, you can't hear what the other witnesses might say so that you aren't potentially influenced by their testimony. Cheryl will be testifying, so please wait here, and we'll let you know when you can enter. It shouldn't take too long. We're pretty sure he will take the plea bargain."

I felt like I was in déja vu and reluctantly sat down. Carla sat next to me. Here we go again," I said. Maybe this will be the last time."

"I hope so," Carla said, wincing in pain from her back. The hard benches were not the most comfortable seats but the only places to sit at the time.

"Even though Bertran said that Richard isn't going to take the plea bargain, I hope he does for Julie's sake."

About half an hour later, everyone emerged suddenly and explosively from the courtroom. Sam's face was filled with frustration. He marched up to Carla and me as we were just standing up.

"He's going to trial," Sam blurted out. "That means we have a lot of work to do to get ready. It won't happen for about four months, but we'll need to get Julie ready to testify. My advocate will be in touch to set up a time for all of us to get together and begin working on things. Do you have any questions?"

It's difficult to ask questions when you feel like you've been run over by a train, and I definitely felt that way. I shook my head, and the DA and his entourage scurried down the hallway.

As we walked down the hallway, it was clear that no one was more shocked than the other. At this point, words seemed futile. We all had the same initial belief that Richard would take the deal. We all thought he wouldn't risk it all and face life in jail for his crime. We were all wrong. Richard was not only willing to risk it all, but he was willing to put everyone else in a position of having to take the stand in front of him and tell their stories, including Julie. His attorney had told him there was no way he could win, but still, they were facing their day in court, which would turn into several days than we imagined. The elevator doors slid open, and we filed into the empty box that took us to the first floor. There was nothing to be said. Was this what Bertran and Richard had hoped for when they spoke with each other and decided not to take the plea? Maybe they thought that by forcing Julie and other family members to testify, the family would elect to have the charges dropped. Perhaps they thought the D.A. would drop the case altogether if the family didn't testify. I shook my head. Richard and Bertran obviously didn't know our family very well. We don't give up, and we don't give in. It would be difficult on us emotionally, but we would fight this and win. Maybe Richard thought he had won on other cases but had never dealt with our family. He would not win this one. The shock and disbelief we felt at Richard's actions were numbing, but they only fueled our determination to fight.

CHAPTER 14

Preparations and More Pleading

❖

The D.A.'s advocate emailed Carla, Sharon, and me, emphasizing the crucial nature of the upcoming meeting to discuss strategy and planning. She asked what date worked best for everyone, and we all eventually agreed on a day and time, fully aware of the significance of our collective decision.

When we arrived, Julie's GAL, who had filed paperwork to be included in the criminal case, was also present at the meeting.

We were all escorted through the maze of offices in the District Attorney's section of the courthouse on the second floor and ended up in a small meeting room big enough for a table and ten chairs.

Carla, Sharon, and I sat on one side of the table while the advocate, Jill, and Sam sat on the other. A police officer was also present to ensure that sensitive matters of the case weren't discussed, as half the room was filled with potential witnesses.

Sam started the meeting. "He chose not to take the last offer we put on the table. He wants to see no more than ten years, but I can't do that."

"We had heard that if he goes to the Department of Corrections, he might never come out," Sharon said. "Are you certain that's not true?"

"You mean, would he get killed in prison?" Sam asked. "Like I said before, I've been doing this for years, and I've never heard of anyone getting killed just because they're a child molester. Have you heard of anything like that on the news?"

No one answered because no one had.

"So what do we do now?" I asked.

"We'll take some time to get to know Julie," Sam said, underlining the necessity of thorough preparation. "Our first meeting with her will be someplace neutral and fun. Maybe we can meet at an ice cream shop downtown. We'll all wear silly T-shirts and just let her get to know who we are. Then we'll take another day to show her the courtroom and let her sit in the big chair. I'll take some time to talk with her and ask her questions. We'll just let her get used to everything a little at a time. Then, before we go to trial, she must have a competency test."

"What does that mean? How is she tested?" Carla asked.

"Well, the judge will put her on the stand and ask her questions to see if she knows the difference between right and wrong, fantasy and reality, and so on."

"What happens if she doesn't pass his test?" I asked, shifting in my chair.

"Then Richard will be released until such a time as the judge feels that Julie's old enough to testify."

The room was quiet. You could hear the buzzing of the fluorescent bulbs overhead.

"Then I guess we'll just have to make sure she's ready," I said. "Is there anything we can do to help prepare her for this?"

"You can begin asking her questions. Does she have a favorite cartoon or character?" Sam asked.

"The characters from Frozen," Sharon said. "Elsa and Anna."

"Maybe begin there. Ask Julie if she thinks that those characters are real. If she says they are, you'll have to start telling her the difference between reality and fantasy."

"She's three years old," I said.

"And she's going to go on the stand to testify. Three years old or not, she needs to know the difference between what's real and what's not."

"Let's move on," I said, trying not to get upset. "Who all are you calling to testify?"

"I'll be calling you three, of course," gesturing to Carla, Sharon, and myself. "Julie's therapist will testify, as will the detective and the forensic interviewer. I'll also be calling your daughter to testify, Stephen."

"Wait. Kaylie?"

"Yes. Kaylie was disclosed to also, wasn't she?"

"Well, yes, but she's in therapy right now for her previous assault ten years ago. Her therapist said that it might harm her to testify in front of Richard and do more harm than good." I was not happy with this situation. "Is there any way she can testify via closed circuit TV or a pre-recorded testimony?"

"No. That won't be possible," Sam said. "She'll need to testify in the courtroom. I'm sorry about any harm it might do to her. Still, if it means the difference between winning and losing my case, we'll have to deal with the consequences afterward."

I'll tell you what, I was furious. Suddenly, this man didn't seem to be on the side of my family anymore. I had to figure out how to get Richard to take that deal. I didn't want my daughter or granddaughter to go through this.

When the meeting was over and we left, I really didn't have much to say. I couldn't get the D.A.'s words out of my head, and despite Carla and Jill trying to reassure me that it would all be okay, I couldn't find comfort in any place they tried pointing me toward. What would you do? I had to figure something out. I needed their support more than ever.

After all of this, I went to the mailbox and had a letter from the courts. I opened it and found that the amended protection order was now in place. Richard could have no contact with Julie nor could he instigate any contact with Sharon either directly or through third parties, Sharon could contact him about his son but not much else. I spoke with Sharon about the situation with the trial and the entire family having to testify.

"You would think that if Richard and his dad felt that this was all a big conspiracy against Richard, he wouldn't even attempt a trial," I said. "I just don't understand. If he loses this, he'll go to jail for 34 years to life. Why didn't he take the plea?"

"I don't know," Sharon said. "I'm going to write to him, though."

Sharon did write to Richard. In her letter, she asked him why he would risk throwing his entire life away on a trial. Then, Sharon did something that she had never done in her life; she begged. She begged Richard not to go ahead with the trial. She told him what her family had been through and what they would have to endure if he continued. She begged him to take the plea bargain so that when the time came, he could still see his son as a child, not as a young man. She begged him to do the right thing.

"I've never begged anyone for anything in my life," she said solemnly.

"I know, sweetheart," I said, giving her a hug. "It really shows how much you love your daughter."

"So you know the real reason I did this?"

"I'm pretty sure you did this so that Julie and Kaylie wouldn't have to testify in court. Am I close?" I asked with a slight smile on my face.

Sharon looked down and smiled. "You know me pretty well, Daddy," she said.

"I guess now we just wait to see what happens," I sighed.

It wasn't long after that when I received another letter from Richard.

There were four typed pages. At first, my stomach churned at the thought of reading what was likely to be a letter filled with ire, but as I started to read, I realized that there was no ire. This letter had a much different tone than the letters that had come before. Richard tried very hard to maintain his composure during the entire communiqué. Richard talked about his son. He spoke about how he really wanted to trust me. Richard told me he was going to accept the plea. He told me that he took the plea because Sharon had written to him and begged him to do so. He said, "I took the plea bargain mainly for 2 reasons. First off, Sharon begged me to take a plea and not throw my life away. She has never begged anything from me, ever. It's extremely humbling, and it broke my heart."

I wasn't sure what to think of this change of attitude that I saw in this young man. It was hard to believe that this was the same person who my granddaughter accused of molesting her. Yet, for every doubt that might have crept into my mind, the image of Julie sitting on her cot and telling her stories chased those images out. I finished reading through the letter and wasn't unpleased. It was a friendly letter. I decided that I would continue to write to Richard.

The next day, I received another letter from Richard. In this one, he apologized for something he had said in the previous letter that might have offended Carla. That was the opening. The remainder of the letter talked about Richard's other son and how charges were being brought against his son's mother for neglect. In my mind, it almost sounded like Richard was hoping that Carla and I could take his son and care for him, but several times, he said he wasn't asking that. It was an interesting letter, and I decided I would need to revisit it sometime. Fortunately, I have maintained all my paperwork from that time.

Richard's sentencing was set for May 14th. What made this incredibly ironic was that on May 14th the year before, Carla and I received the call that Julie was being taken away from Sharon and brought to us. Fate is strange sometimes.

A few days later, when I was working, my cell phone rang, and when I looked, I saw that it was a call from the County Jail. I couldn't take the call since I was on the other phone, so I let it go. I had received a little extra money from a job, so I decided to help Bertran out by putting twenty dollars on Richard's phone account so that they could talk. As I thought about that, I wondered if that was why Richard was calling. Maybe he couldn't reach his dad and was worried.

I tried to call Bertran but couldn't connect to his phone, so on the way back from a meeting, I stopped by to see how he was doing.

When I arrived at the house, I tapped at the screen door. The front door was open, and Bertran yelled, "Come in!"

When I walked in, the first thing I noticed was the very strong smell of pot. Then I saw the pipe sitting next to Bertran. I walked over and sat down.

"What's wrong with your phone?" I asked.

"Oh, Tammy hasn't paid the bill, so it's off. It's a family plan, and she sometimes doesn't get it paid on time. Then I'm without a phone for a day or so," Bertran said.

I had no idea who Tammy was and asked Sharon later. It turned out that Tammy was the girl that Richard had slept with when he received his first sexual offense charge. She lived just down the road from Bertran, and they were good friends.

"Richard tried to call me. I figured he couldn't get through to you and was worried," I said.

"Yeah. That's probably the case. I'm pretty sure it'll be back by tomorrow. I had so many phone calls to make today, too," Bertran was slurring his words a little. "Sorry," he would say, "my neuropathy is acting up."

"You had a lot of phone calls to make?"

"Yes. I have many people who will write letters to the courts on Richard's behalf. We're finding so many holes in this case that has no physical evidence," Bertran was excited.

"We?" I questioned.

"What?" Bertran replied.

"You said 'we're' finding so many holes."

"Yeah," Bertran continued. "Tammy is helping me, and Richard's attorney from the civil case is helping, too. We don't have much time, though. We have to get all of these letters in before the sentencing hearing. Richard's ex's mom is writing a letter to the courts telling them that her daughter also wrote a falsified letter about Richard."

"You've been very busy," I said.

I wasn't sure what to think. I wanted to talk to Sharon about what Bertran was saying.

I called Sharon after I got home.

"Why would Tammy write a letter and be so interested?" Sharon asked.

"I'm not sure," I said, "but apparently, she's doing what she can to get the court's attention."

"Bertran had told me that she was going to write a letter to the courts stating that she never pressed charges and never wanted to," Sharon said.

"I'm not sure that it would matter," I said, "since she was a minor then. He was eighteen, and she was thirteen. It wasn't a matter of choice as much as it was against the law."

"Oh! I have some other news to tell you," Sharon said. "I got to see the video of Julie's interview today. It was hard to hear what she was saying, but it seems they over-exaggerated slightly."

"Did she say that Richard 'tickled' her?"

"Yeah, but she didn't seem very upset about it."

"Well," I said, "at that time, she didn't know it was wrong. I wish I knew who was first to call the authorities."

"I spoke to people at the daycare, and it turns out that she told one of the teachers there."

"Really? What did they tell you?" I needed to hear.

"Julie had been acting strange, so one of the female teachers asked her what was wrong. Julie told her that 'Daddy tickles me down here' and pointed between her legs. They wouldn't have called the police based solely on that statement, but the next thing she said made it so they had to call."

"What did she say?" I asked.

"She told them, 'Don't tell mommy because it will make her mad'."

That statement, it was a cruel blow to my heart. How could someone twist a child's innocence like that? I was weary of this relentless heartbreak, of a life that refused to be normal. But I made a conscious decision. I chose to divert my attention from the bad to the good. I was determined to restore normalcy in my life and emerge as the victor in this battle.

CHAPTER 15

More Court and Police Reports

❖

On this particular morning, I got up as I always did, showered, dressed, and got ready to take the kids to school. I came home, picked up Carla, and headed toward her work.

"What do you have planned for today," Carla asked.

"I'm going to drop you off and then head home. I'm swamped with work and a project that I need to complete by tomorrow, so I'll be able to do that this morning. Then I have a meeting at 11:00 o'clock."

"Are you going to court this morning?"

My heart sank. How could I have forgotten about the crucial court hearing this morning for Julie? And to make matters worse, I had left my phone at home, leaving me in the dark about the rest of the day.

"I forgot about that, but I know I have it on my calendar. Yes, I'm going. I'll let you know what happens. I'm not sure how I will get my stuff done today. Might be a late night."

"I hate it when you must stay up late," Carla said. "I really value the time that we spend together at night."

"I do, too, but I need to get stuff done. Business keeps growing. I need to start scheduling better." I wished I had scheduled better today, but attending court today was important. The hearing would close the civil case in all of this. It was the case that would allow Sharon to have her daughter back for good and not have to have DHS overseeing her every month. Of course, I wanted to be a part of this happy day!

I worked on my project until the very last second, juggling a client's request for video changes. The day felt rushed, and life felt chaotic!

I dashed out to the car, drove downtown, and found a close spot in the parking garage. I sprinted to the courthouse, relieved to have made it just in time.

When his assistant walked through the metal detector, it went crazy. The security guard sighed and took out his wand. I patiently waited and put my keys on the conveyor. It was finally my turn to walk through. I had mastered getting through the metal detector without setting it off, so I ran through, picked up my keys, and sprinted up the stairs.

I checked the docket and saw that I had two minutes before the case was called. I walked into the courtroom and found that all the attorneys, except Richard's attorney, were sitting at the table in front of the Magistrate. I walked quickly to the front of the courtroom, and Sharon's attorney motioned for me to come up and sit next to the GAL. I quietly did so and noticed that Sharon was nowhere to be seen.

The Magistrate spoke matter-of-factly with the attorneys. I learned that Richard's attorney had stepped out of the building, so the Magistrate made small talk, hoping he would return soon, which he finally did.

The Magistrate was ready to order Sharon to get custody of Julie back when she asked Larry's attorney if Larry had any objections.

"Your honor, I haven't seen my client throughout this case. My contact information is incorrect, and I can't find him. I'll try to go through the Probation Department again and see if they know where he is."

Jill was going through several screens on her computer when she said, "Your honor, it would appear that his attorney is not the only one looking for Larry at this time, as he has an active warrant for his arrest, which has been active since December 24th. I'm sure someone will find him."

I found out from Jill later on that the warrant was because Larry hadn't registered as a convicted sex offender.

The Magistrate's decision was a rollercoaster of emotions. She granted Larry's attorney ten days to find him. If he couldn't be located, she would order Julie to be placed with Sharon permanently, with the courts deciding if Larry could see his daughter based on his sex-offensive treatment. This decision left us all in a state of uncertainty and anticipation.

After the court session, Jill had a heart-to-heart with Sharon. She explained that his parental rights could be revoked due to Larry's prolonged absence from Julie's life. She also mentioned that Julie's play therapist was ready to discuss Julie's disclosures. This news left me feeling a mix of concern and determination.

"I didn't think Julie had made any disclosures to the therapist," I said.

"She's made a few specific disclosures," Jill said.

"Would it be okay if I also came to that meeting?" I asked, turning to Sharon. That is if you don't mind. I want to be there if you need support. I'm not sure what would be said, but just in case it's something you haven't heard yet and need a shoulder."

"That's fine, daddy," Sharon said. "I'd like for you to be there. It would probably be a week from Monday. I'll let you know for sure."

"Thank you," I said.

Later that evening, I mentioned this to Carla, who said that she also wanted to be there and asked me to please let her know as soon as I found out when it would be.

The following day was Julie's birthday, a day of joy and celebration amidst the ongoing family struggles. Despite the impending change in custody and the uncertainty it brought, the family was determined to make Julie's day special.

Later that day, I would be in for another surprise, however.

If I were going to be honest with myself, I was tired of surprises. I was tired of this whole thing. I was ready for life to be normal again, and I did not accept that this was the "new normal." I wanted everything to be okay and good and everyone to be happy. I thought about this while driving from a meeting when my phone rang. I looked at it and recognized the number as being from the jail. I took a deep breath and answered the phone.

"Hi, Stephen. Thank you for picking up," I heard Richard say.

"What's up, Richard?" I asked.

"My dad's phone is still not on. Do you know if he's okay?"

I sighed. "I was just over there a few days ago because I was also concerned. He's fine. Tammy hasn't paid his bill, so the phone is not working."

I was very close to Bertran's home, so I decided to swing by while I had Richard on the phone. I thought that Bertran would appreciate being able to speak to his son, so I made a slight detour and was in front of Bertran's home within a minute.

"I just pulled up in front of your dad's house. I'll run up and see if he's home so you can talk to him." I knew that Bertran wouldn't be anywhere else, and sure enough, when he approached the front door, the storm door was closed, but the front door was open.

I knocked at the door and heard Bertran yell, "Come in!"

I walked in with the phone still to my ear. Once again, the house smelled strongly of pot, and Bertran was sitting in his recliner watching movies on his phone.

"Hey!" Bertran said with a smile. "What are you doing here?"

"Here," I said, handing my phone to Bertran. "Speak with your son."

Bertran looked confused. "My son?" He took the phone, put it to his ear, and repeated, "My son?"

I figured the conversation would last for some time, but I was wrong. Bertran mentioned the letters and what he was doing and then handed the phone back to me. I didn't see any compassion or familial love between the two. I said goodbye to Bertran and walked away. I put the phone up to my ear, and Richard was still there.

"Well, there you go. Your dad is doing okay. I'm sure he'll have his phone back on soon."

"Thanks, Stephen. I feel better now."

Richard went on to talk about the letters he had sent me and apologized for not being so nice in some of them. He talked about his son being taken away from his Ex. He talked about things that he probably wished he could have talked to his dad about. Then, the automated timer announced one minute was remaining, and we said, "Goodbye."

My heart was touched. I understood that this father-and-son relationship was not good and probably never had been. I knew that my own relationship between me and my father was not a good one. In fact, I hadn't heard from my father in over six years despite my efforts to contact him, so I knew what Richard must have been going through. Still, it didn't excuse what Richard had done. My distance from my father had made me a kind man and, I hoped, a better father to my children.

As Julie's birthday party approached, the anticipation and excitement in the family were palpable. We were all eager to see how she was doing and to celebrate this special day with her.

On Saturday, the entire family was ready to celebrate. We met Julie and Sharon at the movie theatre, and the joy and laughter filled the air. We had a great time together, and Julie's excitement was contagious. She loved the movie and was thrilled about the ice cream treat that awaited us. I noticed that her stuttering seemed to be getting worse, and I couldn't help but wonder if it had anything to do with her traumas or if it was just the way she was growing up. Julie, my granddaughter, had been through a lot, and I was always concerned about her well-being. I would never know.

Only a few days later, Sharon texted me. She was at the police station attempting to pick up the police report that none of our family had seen. This report was crucial as it contained information about Julie's past that could help us understand her better. A few minutes later, my phone rang. It was Sharon.

"So, were you able to get the police report?" I asked.

"No," Sharon said. "They had sent me a letter saying that I could come down and pick it up. When I got to the police station, they got a report and told me it would cost $9.75. It turned out that the report which they gave me wasn't for Julie at all, so they took it back and refunded my money. Then they told me they had to carefully review the report to ensure I could get it since Julie was originally taken from me."

"Huh," I replied, not knowing what to make of it all. "I wonder if the police would give it to me because your mom and I had custody for a while?" It was a rhetorical question, really, but I still wondered.

It didn't matter, as Sharon got the report two days later.

I had wished we had access to this report much earlier, or at least the information it contained. After reading it, things turned for both Sharon and me.

Sharon texted me, "If you're not busy, do you want to meet me at the police station? I'm going to pick up the police report."

I didn't get the text until I got home. I had been trying hard not to answer texts while driving. I had just dropped off Carla at work and was on my way home. When I arrived and read Sharon's text, I answered.

"I just got back from taking mom to work. Where are you now?"

Sharon answered, "Police station parking lot…I just got it."

I said, "Oh cool! Big file?"

"Oh yeah!" Sharon responded.

It was quiet for a little while, and then Sharon texted me again. This one didn't sound good.

"…I hope he leaves when he gets out. I haven't had an anxiety attack like this in a long time."

I became very concerned. I texted back, "Oh, do you need to come visit? Can you call me?"

My phone rang moments later. "What's going on, sweetheart? Would it help to talk about it?"

"I can only imagine how overwhelming it must be to learn all this from the report. It's like finally seeing what everyone was trying to show you, right?"

"Like what? I can hear from the sound of your voice you're really upset. Is it like what everyone told you but you couldn't see before?"

"Yeah. Pretty much like that. I found out that Julie told the daycare pretty much the story that she told you and told them not to tell me. There are all sorts of stories that she told people that we had no idea were told. I can't believe the things that Richard did. I wish that I had known this was going on."

"Oh, sweetheart. I'm so sorry it's hitting you this way, but it's probably good. Now you can finally see what everyone was seeing before. You should bring it by when you can, and I'll make a copy. Then, if you ever decide to rip certain parts to shreds, you can do so and still know that you have a replacement copy here."

"That's a brave and wise decision, Sharon. Reading the report before your therapy appointment might help you process it better. You're doing great."

"Good thinking!" I said. "Smart girl."

I hung up the phone and texted Carla, filling her in on the recently revealed events. She could step outside from where she was working and call me.

I explained everything Sharon had told me, and Carla was glad Sharon could finally see the big picture. Sharon decided to stay with a friend that night so that she could get help with the kids, also indicating that she didn't think it was a good idea to be alone.

The next day, I sat at my desk working on a few projects when the front door opened.

"Knock, knock," came the familiar voice as Sharon entered the front room.

"How are you doing, sweetheart?" I asked with a smile, trying to mask my concern. Sharon's arrival had caught me off guard, and I was unsure how to react.

"It's Been better, it's been worse," she said, handing me the thick pile of papers comprising the police report.

I wanted to whistle. It was a lot bigger than Kaylie's file had been. I took it and placed it in the auto-feeder on my copier. Sharon spoke more about the report and how, even though some names were blacked out, she was pretty sure she knew whom they belonged to.

"So when Bertran and Richard told us things on this report, were they accurate?" I asked.

"Only a little, but for most of what they said to us, no."

Suddenly, I didn't feel as charitable as I had. I had trusted too much, given too many chances, and let my feelings be manipulated. Did I feel foolish? I felt foolish times a hundred. I felt like he had been made a fool of me, not just once but every time I spoke with Richard or Bertran. Every time. I wondered how many times that was. I shook my head and didn't want to think about it, but I did wonder what people thought about me being as sympathetic as I had been toward Richard. Another wave of foolishness washed over me. No more. I was done being foolish and done being fooled. I had a victim impact statement to write for the court, and I was sure I knew what would be said.

When the copy of the report had been made, I picked up the first page and started to read. I read how the daycare was concerned about Julie and how she told them her story of how daddy tickled her when they were on the couch and how she didn't like it. She told the teachers where he would tickle her and told her not to tell her mommy. I had to put the report down momentarily as my eyes filled with tears. It never seems to get any easier, I thought to myself. The weight of the situation was heavy on my heart, and I wondered how I would get through the entire thirty-or-so-page report. I wanted to know everything that happened. Unfortunately, I had a two-hour drive that evening to a job. I wouldn't be back until around midnight, so the report would have to wait until tomorrow. I sighed, put the report on Carla's and my bed so she could read it when she got home, and packed the car to leave.

My trust in humanity had been shattered. This was just one more thing to chalk up to these wreckers of lives. I only hoped that they were done ruining the lives of my family. I felt a deep sense of betrayal and disillusionment, wondering how people could be capable of such cruelty. It was a stark reminder of the darker side of human nature, a side I had always tried to ignore.

CHAPTER 16

The Big Picture

❖

When I arrived home that evening from my job, it was close to midnight, and Carla was in bed with her reading light on. I walked over and kissed her and saw that she was reading the police report. I went into the bathroom and got ready for bed.

I climbed into bed and looked at where Carla was in the report. She was reading the last few pages, which were from Julie's therapist and explained what had been disclosed to her during therapy. I wanted to read the rest of the report in order, so I didn't read over her shoulder.

When she was done, she put the report down and turned off the light.

"I didn't realize it would take so long to read," she said.

"It seems pretty detailed," I said in the dark.

"I just can't believe everything that he did. Everything that Julie revealed."

Carla turned over. I said "goodnight" and started to drift off to sleep when Carla blurted out, "Why can't I get these images out of my head? I can't believe what he did to her."

"I haven't read it yet, so I'm not sure what part you're talking about, although I imagine the entire report will be an eye-opener."

Carla turned over and looked at me in the faint light from the streetlights shining in through the window. "You haven't read it? I thought you had."

"I started to after I copied it, but before I could get past the first few pages, I had to leave. I'll read it this weekend. Do you need to talk about it, though?" I was concerned about how this report would affect my family. We had already been through so much. I hoped this would put any questions to rest and start the healing process.

"No, I'll let you read it first," Carla said, turning back over.

Over the next few days, my schedule was busy with more trips out of town. It wasn't until Sunday rolled around that I was able to sit back down and, with some trepidation, begin reading the report again.

I was impressed, now seeing the big picture, with the speed and efficiency of how the entire case was handled. From my personal perspective, it seemed to drag on, but things actually moved very quickly in the background. When the daycare notified the police about Julie's disclosure, they responded by going to Sharon's apartment that evening.

The two officers who went with the caseworker wrote about the visit to the apartment, and the officer who interviewed Richard provided more detail. One very noticeable item was how nervous Richard was. The officer said that Richard's "eyes were opened wide while I spoke with him, and he was visibly shaking, particularly in his legs."

The report talked about them bringing Julie to our house and how we were informed about the upcoming court hearings and interviews for Julie.

The next section in the report summarized the forensic interview with Julie. As I read this, I could see that Julie shut down after hearing the noise that she thought was "Daddy" outside of the interview room door, but she did manage to tell about the tickling. It was difficult for me to read this, but I continued on. With each word, I felt more and more played by Richard and Bertran.

I turned the page to the next section and read Sharon's interview with the detective. I was proud of how my daughter was honest about her feelings and open with her thoughts. Then I read the detective's interview with Richard.

The detective was asking questions along the same lines which I would have asked. Something could have happened. It might have been poor judgment on Richard's part. Therapy would help. However, Richard would respond defensively and maintain that he didn't do anything and would never do anything. He refused the lie detector test, saying that his anxiety disorder would make all of his answers inconclusive. When the detective said they had a test that analyzed the voice, Richard decided it would be best to consult with an attorney. He also indicated that Julie could easily be led into a conversation. Still, when the detective said she had been forensically interviewed with no leading questions, Richard said he wasn't impressed and wanted a lawyer.

I thought about this section. I had never heard what Richard had said in his interview. He certainly had the right answers, but they were almost too perfect and well-timed, like an actor who had memorized his lines and knew what to say and when. I recalled telling Richard that maybe he had made a mistake and just needed to see a therapist. Richard's answer to that statement was silence.

I went to the next section.

This next section brought tears to my eyes yet again. It was regarding Carla telling the caseworker and the detective about another disclosure that Julie had made, where Richard would make her sit on him when he wouldn't wear pants, and have her move her hips back and forth. Julie said it would make her grumpy. While she was telling Carla this, Julie cried and hugged her not wanting to let go. Julie said she couldn't tell mommy because it would make her cry. It made me cry.

I moved on to the next section.

This section reflected the interview given to my daughter, Kaylie. I had to take a break when Kaylie told the interviewer that she remembered being in the same interview room when she was four. Knowing what Kaylie was currently going through hurt my heart. I love my daughter so much and wish that life hadn't dealt her this blow. I took a deep breath and continued reading.

In her interview, Kaylie bravely shared how Julie would talk with her at night after the lights were off and what Richard would do to her. At one point, Kaylie recounted a dream that Julie shared about how she smashed Richard, and he wouldn't talk to her anymore. She demonstrated what that meant by hitting a stuffed animal. Her courage in sharing these painful memories is truly commendable.

With each section I read, I became sadder but more determined to understand the situation. The big picture was truly falling together, and I was committed to seeing it through.

The following section includes my interview with the detective. I relived the interview and realized that it was very accurate. The detective's thorough work and accurate report reassured me that what I was reading was correct. I made a mental note to send everyone involved in this case a big "Thank You" for keeping my granddaughter safe and stopping this before it could go any further.

The following section was one page and two sentences. The DA had accepted the case, and a warrant was drawn up.

The following section includes information from the second interview between Sharon and the detective.

Cheryl spoke with Sharon about Richard. Sharon told how Richard would show up unannounced at her work and school. How he had threatened suicide. How he talked about the police not having any evidence. How Sharon should support him, and how she should stand up for him. She told Cheryl how Richard said he still loved Sharon and Julie and wanted their family back together again. There was so much that Richard said and did that indicated that he tried to control the situation by controlling Sharon. Sharon believed Julie. Why would a three-year-old make this up?

Good for you! I thought.

The following section contained an email I sent to Cheryl about what Julie had disclosed to me.

The following section provides details of another interview conducted at the daycare about Julie. Since there was no new information here, I moved on.

The next section discussed Julie's medical records and what, if anything, had been found in them. This part must remain confidential.

The report continued forever, but it was a vast and complex case. I looked. There were only a few pages left.

The following section discusses another interview with the daycare and an update on Julie's behavior. I was concerned about the reported behavior and wondered if having Julie and Sharon over to the house more often would be a good idea. I had wanted that anyway. I missed seeing my family and felt that the happiness found within the walls of my home was good therapy for my extended family no longer living with me. More mental notes.

The following section tells how the detective downloaded the calls made by Richard while in jail. Twenty-six calls were made and logged into the system for evidence. I was deeply grateful for the detective's thoroughness and dedication to the case. Her actions were a testament to the justice system's commitment to protecting the innocent.

I reached the final two pages of the report. These included statements from Julie's therapist, more disclosures and behaviors, and the "images" that Carla wanted to purge from her mind that night. I knew that I would be visiting this therapist the following day and would hear in her own words what I had just read and possibly more. I decided to wait until I listened to what had to be said before journaling more.

But now it was time to forgive myself for being fooled many times. I had always been taught to forgive quickly and love my fellow human beings. I had been taken for a ride and didn't like it. I was done. As much as this review of the entire case had affected me, I had no idea how much the therapist's words the next day would shake me to my core.

CHAPTER 17

The Therapist

❖

In the afternoon, Carla, Sharon, and I met at the therapist's office. We waited in the waiting room while the therapist prepared to meet us.

After what seemed like a long wait, she entered the waiting room. "How are you guys doing?" she asked, smiling. "Come on back."

We stood and followed Doctor Rawlins back to her office.

We entered a large but comfortable room, where Carla and I sat on the sofa. Sharon sat in a comfy chair, and Darla, Julie's therapist, sat in a corner where she could address us all.

Dr. Rawlins, Julie's therapist, clarified her role in Julie's therapy. She wasn't there to form opinions but to observe and take notes while Julie played. Her task was to discern if something had happened and to note any specific behaviors that might indicate this.

Sharon, Carla, and I listened as Darla went through her notes. She talked about how Julie would be angry at the anatomically correct male dolls. She would point to their genitals and say, "I don't like that…" and then throw the doll across the room. They learned that Julie knew the correct names for male body parts. This surprised Sharon, as she didn't know where Julie had learned this information.

Other events happened, and Julie would talk about the need to protect her mom from the bad man or the monsters. She would always tell Darla that she needed to lock the door to the playroom before they started playing.

Julie's protective and fearful nature became more apparent as the session progressed. Darla recounted an incident where Julie, upon seeing a male therapist who resembled Richard, immediately sought refuge behind Darla, clutching onto her legs in fear. This incident highlighted Julie's deep-seated fear and her need for protection.

"Julie saw him and immediately hid behind me," Darla said. "She clutched onto my legs and was afraid. I asked her what was wrong, and she pointed to the male therapist and said, 'I don't like him. He's a scary man,' at which point we went back down, and the male therapist, seeing what was going on, went back upstairs and out of sight."

The four of us met for almost an hour and a half. When the meeting was over, I had no doubt about what happened and who did it. The weight of uncertainty was finally lifted, and I felt a profound sense of closure. I couldn't believe it took me this long to finally reach 100% surety about where the lies came from.

I wasn't angry at the lies. I understood that people lied to protect themselves. I understood that Richard didn't want to go to prison and that Bertran didn't want to see his son go to jail. I understood that they felt that if they could keep me as an ally and had someone like me who would be on their side, things might go easier for Richard. I understood that the survival instinct in people was strong. Still, I also understood that my instinct to protect my family was stronger than anything these two could break. Now that I knew the whole truth, I felt sorry for Richard. I didn't feel sorry for him because he was going to prison, but I felt sorry for him for being unable to admit the truth to those around him. I had no idea whether Richard could admit the truth to himself, but I hoped so. That would be the only way that he could ever truly heal. I suspected not healing would be much like spending your life in a living hell. Now, I had to think of a way to help myself to recover from all of this.

CHAPTER 18

Sentencing

❖

There were only a few weeks until sentencing. The family felt an air of relief. There would finally be some closure to this, at least for now.

However, the story was far from over. There were still a few unexpected twists waiting to unfold. To everyone's surprise, Sharon had a court appearance, and Carla accompanied her. She had not been served any papers and only discovered her obligation to be there when she stumbled upon her and Richard's names on the court schedule while looking for a different date and time.

She and Carla arrived at the courthouse that morning and checked the docket. Sure enough, her name was there, so they went into the empty courtroom and sat down.

They waited for what seemed like a very long time, but in reality, it was only about 10 minutes. Eventually, the court clerk stuck her head in the room from the back and looked surprised to see the two women sitting there. "Oh!" she exclaimed, "We'll be in shortly."

The door quickly closed, and within a few minutes, a buzzer sounded, and the clerk stepped in. "All rise," she said.

Carla and Sharon stood as the judge entered the room and sat at her bench.

"You may be seated," the judge said, amused at the small gathering. She looked over her notes and then up at the two women sitting in the gallery. "Miss Bolton," she said, looking at Sharon, "why don't you come and sit on this side of the railing so that it's easier to speak with you and easier for the clerk to hear what you have to say?"

Sharon sat in the chair where she would typically sit.

"It seems that we're here today to discuss the addition of Mr. Pantane to his son's birth certificate," the judge stated, her words carrying the weight of her authority.

"Your honor," Sharon said, "I didn't even know I was supposed to be here today. I saw it when I was looking for a different court hearing time. I haven't received any papers or been contacted by anyone."

The judge raised her eyebrows. "Really? Well, I'll have the clerk give you a copy of the petition while we get Mr. Pantane on the phone."

The clerk brought Sharon some papers, and the judge tried to get through to the jail. The first connection was not good, so she had to call back. When she finally got through, she started speaking with Richard.

"Mr. Pantane, it has come to the court's attention that Miss Bolton has not had sufficient time to read the paperwork you filed. It would seem that you didn't have her served properly. She needs time to respond to your petition."

"I'm incarcerated," Richard snarled. "I can't do that."

"Well, Mr. Pantane," the judge replied smiling, "I believe you could have done so, even from jail. You were able to file your petition from jail, and I believe you could have followed the correct procedure. Seeing this is the case, I will continue this hearing until early June to give Miss Bolton time to review your paperwork and respond if she wants to." This decision relieved Sharon and brought anxiety to Richard, extending the uncertainty and the legal process.

"Your honor," Richard said, "I don't even know where I'll be in early June. This isn't fair." His frustration could be heard in his voice.

Sharon's amusement was evident as she realized Richard had tried to sneak this into the legal system without an attorney.

"Mr. Pantane, why won't you know where you'll be in early June?" The judge's calm response contrasted with Richard's frustration, and Sharon stifled a smile.

"Because I'm going to be sentenced soon, and the last time I went to DOC, they had me waiting in a county jail somewhere for a few weeks before they moved me." Richard was getting irritated.

"It will be up to you, Mr. Pantane, to be sure that you keep this court informed as to your whereabouts so that we can contact you on the day of the hearing," the judge said matter-of-factly.

"I don't think I can do that," Richard said, exasperated. "I don't know where I will be."

"Mr. Pantane. You must contact this court when moving to a new facility. I'm sure that you'll be able to do that. This case is continued until June 5th at 9 o'clock in the morning."

At that point, the phone line went dead. Carla was pretty sure that it wasn't because the judge hung up. The judge pursed her lips and looked out at Sharon, smiling again. "Will that date work for you, Miss Bolton?"

"It should unless I have a class that day."

At that point, Carla broke in and told Sharon, "Don't worry about it. We'll make it work."

Over the next week, I noticed that I had several missed calls from the county jail on my phone. I was in a busy time of the year, working long hours and unable to take many calls. I could return calls but was seldom available to answer my phone. Perhaps Richard was trying to call me to discuss why Sharon wasn't signing the paperwork. I had always taught my children to never sign anything before reading it. I was proud of Sharon for following my example.

While it was difficult for me to answer my phone during this busy time, in addition, my health was beginning to go downhill. I didn't say anything to anyone about my pain and the strange feelings

I was starting to get inside. My eyes weren't doing well, and I was beginning to get infections in them, making it hard for me to see at times. I fulfilled my promise to Richard that I had made a few weeks earlier, and I sent him a short letter and some photos of his son from Easter. I hadn't heard from Bertran in weeks. However, I did hear that Richard's old girlfriend, who first got him in trouble with the law, was still in love with Richard and was doing everything she could to help him, blaming his situation on the family he had wronged.

I went on with my life and then realized, on a cloudy and cold Wednesday morning, that in less than twenty-four hours, I would once again be sitting in a courtroom and listening to the judge as Richard was sentenced for his crime.

I was concerned not only for my granddaughter's future but also wondered how Richard would be after sitting in prison for years, thinking about the people who had done this to him, in his mind anyway, but in reality, he had done this to himself. I hoped that Richard would be thinking about how he could get better. But I didn't know what he was thinking and that no one had an answer to that except Richard. I knew that only time would tell. In the meantime, I had to get on with my life and at least get on with the work that was before me today. Tomorrow was another day and the beginning of that adventure. I would wait to see what that day would bring.

That night, neither Carla nor I slept well. Carla was trying to decide whether to speak in court, but I tossed and turned, wondering what would happen the next day.

When we woke up the next morning, I had taken the kids to school, and Carla had taken the day off from work. It all started out as a normal day. Then, it was time to leave for court.

Carla and I arrived at the courthouse and found the courtroom where the hearing would be held. We sat outside on the hard benches, waiting for Sharon to arrive. When she did come, she had a friend with her for moral and emotional support. We all chatted briefly and then went into the courtroom to sit down.

I was surprised to find Richard already inside and seated against the wall. He stood out in his orange jumpsuit and shackles. Another inmate sat beside him, waiting for his turn before the judge. As fate would have it, the other inmate would go first.

This particular hearing went very quickly; before I knew it, it was time for Richard to be heard. The DA, who was once again a different person than we had met before, had come over and asked if anyone in the family wanted to say anything to the court. I shook my head. I knew that Richard had received my latest letter and I had said everything I wanted Richard to know. I had nothing more to say. Sharon had nothing to say at this point. I found out later that Carla wanted to speak, but the DA turned away after seeing Sharon and I shake our heads.

The judge said, "This is a sentencing hearing for Richard Pantane. I have read all of the pre-sentencing letters both for Mr. Pantane and from the family, so I would now like to hear from the DA in this case."

Richard's attorney stood. "Before the DA speaks, your honor, I would like to correct a few things that were reported incorrectly on the Psycho-sexual evaluation report."

"Go ahead, Mr. Carlson," the judge said, and Carlson walked up to the podium to speak.

"There are several things, your honor, that we would like to correct in the report. First of all, Mr. Pantane never said that he wanted to kill the people responsible for putting him in jail. Instead, he said that he wanted to kill the person who did this to his daughter. Additionally, your honor, he never called the interviewer a 'bitch' as he would never speak with someone in authority in that manner."

Mr. Carlson continued with another twenty-eight disputes. Once he was done, the judge thanked him and returned to the sentencing.

"Mr. Mercer," he said to the DA, "please address the court."

The DA stood up and took his file to the podium. He opened the file, read some papers for a moment, and then started to speak.

"Your honor, Mr. Pantane is a repeat sexual offender. He has shown time and time again that he takes no responsibility for anything that happens to him. Instead, he blames everything and everyone else. It's never his fault. He had his attorney make corrections in his evaluation report. Are we to believe that professional, court-appointed workers can make many mistakes or even lie on their reports?" The DA continued to talk about Richard's past history and how he had even failed on three occasions to register as a sex offender. "My purpose today is not to imprison Mr. Pantane for his actions but to protect society and others from his future crimes. My purpose today is to ensure he doesn't perpetrate again and protect the public. It's not a matter of if he will offend again, but when."

Mr. Mercer sat down. The judge then looked at Mr. Carlson and said, "Mr. Carlson?"

Richard's attorney walked to the podium and looked at his file. "Your honor, Mr. Pantane has been a victim of circumstance. It's not that he refuses to take responsibility for his actions. In fact, he's here today because he is taking responsibility. He didn't lie to the professionals; instead, they made mistakes in putting down what he said. Mr. Pantane is a good person with a good heart."

Carlson continued telling the judge what he thought the judge wanted to hear to reduce the sentence to a minimum and then sat down.

Next, the judge addressed Richard. "Would you like to say anything, Mr. Pantane?"

"Yes, your honor," Richard said. He stood and walked over to the podium.

"Your honor, I have written out what I want to say. I thought a lot about this, and I have a few pages. Is that okay?"

"Take your time, Mr. Pantane," the judge said.

"Thank you, your honor," Richard said, looking down at his letter.

"Your honor, I could never do anything like what I have been accused of. It tears me up that my family has had to go through what they have been put through. I never wanted them to go through any of this." Richard's voice was shaking, and it was evident, even from behind him, that he was beginning to cry. "I love my family. I would never, ever do anything to hurt any of them. I would do anything for them. I have taken evaluations that have been degrading and that no person should ever have to go through. My credibility and my reputation have been ruined. I have tried hard to make a good life and reach a point where I could have a family and care for them, and now that is all gone because of someone who hurt my little girl."

I heard Carla crying, and Sharon was also crying. I felt Carla turn around to comfort our daughter. I continued to listen to Richard talk about his bad luck and how life had not been good to him. At some point, I realized that neither Carla nor Sharon were crying anymore. I listened more to Richard.

"I can't believe what my wife and daughter have been through. The only reason that I took the plea bargain was because Sharon begged me to not throw my life away and never be there for my son. My family needs me, and I want to be there for them, so I'd rather go to jail to keep the family together and be able to go back to them sooner than never."

During the entire hearing, Bertran never showed up. I felt terrible that Richard's own father didn't show up to say anything to comfort his son. I would find out later why that was.

When Richard was done, he sat back down next to his attorney. It was quiet for a few moments. Then the judge spoke.

'Mr. Pantane seems to be a very intelligent person, a good writer, and an excellent speaker. I have heard from all parties, and since Mr. Pantane's father hasn't arrived, I'm ready to proceed. The plea bargain called for ten to fourteen years. I'm going to split the difference. On count one, Richard was sentenced to twelve years in the Department of Corrections with three years of mandatory parole. On count two, he received a three-year concurrent sentence with two years of mandatory parole. The judge, considering Richard's non-violent sexual predator status, deemed this to be the most appropriate sentencing.

Everyone stood. The deputy escorted Richard out of the courtroom. Carla, Sharon, Sharon's friend, and I made our way to the door. As soon as we reached the outer door of the courtroom, Sharon started running down the hallway toward the bathroom. Her friend followed quickly.

Carla turned to me. "I'm going to make sure that she's okay. Why don't you stay and talk with the DA."

Carla walked quickly toward the bathroom, and I turned to see the DA standing only inches away from me.

"Do you have any questions for me?" the DA asked me.

"Not that I can think of," I said, "but thank you for everything you did."

"Okay, well, I have another courtroom to be in, so if you have any questions, please contact the advocate."

The DA shook my hand and walked off.

I walked down to the restrooms and sat down. People say that when you come to the end of a major life crisis, it feels like the weight of the world has been lifted from your shoulders. I had never really thought about it before, but at this moment, I actually felt physically lighter. It was literally as if a weight had been lifted. I was worried about Sharon and wondered what was going on. I hoped that she wasn't devastated by the recent events.

Soon, Carla, Sharon, and Sharon's friend left the bathroom. At the same time, the DA advocate walked up and started talking with Carla. Sharon and her friend were talking, and I wanted to give her that moment.

I turned to join the conversation with Carla and the advocate.

"I can make sure that you know Richard's status at all times," she told Carla, "and if you need help with continuing the protective order after he's released, hopefully, I'll still be here, and I can help you with that as well."

"Thank you," Carla said. "We'll be in touch."

We all left for the elevator. The advocate left on her floor, and Carla, Sharon, Sharon's friend, and I left the building. Sharon and her friend went to their car and Carla and I to ours.

"Was Sharon okay?" I asked Carla.

"Yeah," Carla said. "When I got to the bathroom, Sharon was in a stall. She came out and blew her nose, but she wasn't crying. She just had to use the bathroom. Sharon, like me, was sad when Richard started reading his letter. Then, seemingly at the same time, we both stopped. We realized that Richard was saying things to get sympathy from the judge. We actually both became angry when he started calling Sharon his wife and Julie, his daughter. We probably wouldn't have become angry if he hadn't gone on for so long. Still, after a certain point, it became obvious that he was saying whatever he could to gain sympathy."

I thought about the speech and realized that she was right. But now it was over, right?

That evening, I had a job to do. As I was driving to the job, my phone rang. I looked at it and realized that it was from the jail.

I answered the phone and heard Richard's voice. His plea for me to check on his dad, despite everything that had happened, stirred a mix of emotions in me.

"Can you please go check on my dad?" Richard pleaded. "He's in the hospital with heart failure. That's why he wasn't there today. I talked to him but only briefly."

"Yes, I can do that for you," I said.

Then Richard began talking about things that had happened and what I said in his letter. He spoke of the mysterious friend who had turned him in and how he and Sharon had talked about child abuse in front of Julie within twenty-four hours of her disclosing to the daycare. This put a little doubt in my mind, so when I got home, I asked Sharon about everything that Richard had said to me.

"I don't recall ever talking about that in front of Julie or at all," Sharon said.

Once again, I was almost taken in but disproved what was being told.

I did call Bertran and found out that he was in the hospital and being prepped for an internal heart defibrillator. I decided to go and see him at the hospital in a few days, but as far as I knew, he never received any surgeries.

Now, it was over.

After a few weeks, the phone calls stopped. Bertran stopped calling me, and eventually, I found out that he had moved out of state.

Richard sent me four more letters before he was transferred to a state prison. In one of them, he made an interesting statement.

When we were first married, Carla worked for a local organization where she was a victim's advocate for teenagers who had troubled lives and/or had been sexually assaulted. She mentioned this in her victim's impact statement.

Richard wrote that if he had known before he started dating Sharon that Carla had been a victim's advocate, he would never have dated her. He mentioned that she only cares about the victims and, later in the letter, claimed that he had been a victim of sexual assault when he was younger.

I had to think about this. Did this mean that he knew in advance that there would be a victim in the family once he became involved with them? It was a strange thought, but it seemed to fit what was being said.

I haven't heard from him since he was transferred to the state facility.

Bertran no longer contacts me at all.

CHAPTER 19

The Case, But Not the Story

❖

When all was said and done, everyone except Richard went home. I sat down and wrote in my journal about my feelings. This is what I wrote:

"I would like to think that this is a happy ending. I would like to believe that we're all done with this. If I genuinely thought that, I would be in denial and lying. In my life, I have seen sexual assault victims much later, after their assaults, and I know that this is not the end. My wife and two of my daughters were assaulted. There are many good times, but there are also lingering effects of great sadness, guilt, depression, blame, shame, and a host of other emotions that I probably will never be able to fully comprehend.

I've watched my wife cringe at movies when violent assaults are portrayed. I've seen my daughters go through guilt and blame and confusion at what happened to them and ask, 'Am I to blame for all of this?' A happy ending? This isn't a board game where, when the game is over, it's over. It's life. It continues to continue. Each encounter and each situation creates a moment of doubt and, sometimes, fear. A simple relationship turns into a guessing game of who should be trusted. Each failure results in a questioning of one's abilities. This is not the end. In a few years, Julie may be back in therapy, wondering why she can't relate to boys or girls in an intimate setting. In sexual assault or molestation, there is no happy ending, and there won't be until it's stopped. How can it be stopped? It's up to each of us to report any assaults to the proper authorities. I'm not saying that each of us should start a witch-hunt, but each and every one of us should be vigilant and watch for signs. If those signs are present, take action! Don't think that you can handle the situation by yourself. Only professionals can reach the results that we all want to see. It's easy to make excuses and say that no one will understand, ask what the neighbors will think, or will the school teacher think that I'm a terrible parent because I allowed this to happen. The worst train of thought is that it will all just go away. It will never go away until we teach people that this is wrong! Take action. Don't be afraid. Be more fearful of not taking action. We need to end this now and not wait until tomorrow. The future of our children and our loved ones relies on what we do today. We made it through this but still have a long way to go. Don't let it get as far as we did. Be as brave as the three-year-old in this story. Tell!"

CHAPTER 20

Ten Years Later

❖

Here we are, ten years later. Julie is a resilient thirteen-year-old and has returned to therapy. She's navigating her sexual orientation, leaning towards women, and bravely facing a past she can't fully remember.

Carla and I moved from our hometown. While we are only half an hour away, we still don't see the kids as often as we would like. Family gatherings happen during holidays and birthdays.

Sharon is stuck in another abusive relationship. It continues no matter how Carla and I encourage her to get out of it.

Kaylie, with a kind and loving boyfriend, is at a turning point in her life. She's ready to confront her past, and we're hopeful for her future. She has become a wonderful and loving soul. Her boyfriend is kind and funny, and Carla and I love him as much as one of our own children.

We love all our children unconditionally, supporting them in every way we can. We are, and always will be, their parents.

Richard is out of prison. He was released this year. He had told me he would settle far away from Sharon, but he lives only a few miles away from her and her family. He sends me texts, and I answer because I want to know where he is and his state of mind. He has still never admitted his guilt, nor has he offered an apology for anything he did. He has violated the protection order, still in place, by sending Sharon an email. She did not respond.

He has a car. He says he has a job but cannot tell me what it is. I don't know much about his life now, and I don't want to know. Sometimes, he asks me to send him pictures of his son. I'm waiting for Sharon to contact his Parole Officer to find out if that's even allowed.

I haven't heard from Bertran in years. He occasionally likes something on my social media posts, so I know he's still around.

Richard's Mother hasn't reached out at all since Richard left prison.

I hope this book has helped you in some way.

ABOUT THE AUTHOR

Drew Bankston lives in the Rocky Mountains with his wife, two amazing dogs, and a garden.

Before he started writing, Drew received his bachelor's degree in Bio-Ag Sciences from Colorado State University. He worked various jobs in retail and Asset Protection through the years while writing and creating some pretty cool stories. He's a Certified Forensic Interviewer with advanced training in that field.

He's still working for others but would eventually like to write full-time and share more of his imagination with everyone. His focus is to release six fantastic books per year and watch his library of new stories grow!

If you want to know when Drew's next book will come out, please visit his website at http://www.drewbankston.com, where you can sign up to receive an email in advance of his next release.

www.ingramcontent.com/pod-product-compliance
Lightning Source LLC
Chambersburg PA
CBHW020001290326
41935CB00007B/261